The Vitality of Liberation Theology

Missional Church, Public Theology, World Christianity

Stephen Bevans, Paul S. Chung, Veli-Matti Kärkkäinen
and Craig L. Nessan, Series Editors

IN THE MIDST OF globalization there is crisis as well as opportunity. A model of God's mission is of special significance for ecclesiology and public theology when explored in diverse perspectives and frameworks in the postcolonial context of World Christianity. In the face of the new, complex global civilization characterized by the Second Axial Age, the theology of mission, missional ecclesiology, and public ethics endeavor to provide a larger framework for missiology in interaction with our social, multicultural, political, economic, and intercivilizational situation; they create ways to refurbish mission as constructive theology in critical and creative engagement with cultural anthropology, world religions, prophetic theology, postcolonial hermeneutics, and contextual theologies of World Christianity. Such endeavors play a critical role in generating theological, missional, social-ethical alternatives to the reality of Empire—a reality characterized by civilizational conflict, and by the complex system of a colonized lifeworld that is embedded within practices of greed, dominion, and ecological devastation. This series—Missional Church, Public Theology, World Christianity—invites scholars to promote alternative church practices for life-enhancing culture and for evangelization as telling the truth in the public sphere, especially in solidarity with those on the margins and in ecological stewardship for the lifeworld.

The Vitality of Liberation Theology

CRAIG L. NESSAN

Foreword by Paul S. Chung

◥PICKWICK *Publications* · Eugene, Oregon

THE VITALITY OF LIBERATION THEOLOGY

Missional Church, Public Theology, World Christianity 3

Copyright © 2012 Craig L. Nessan. All rights reserved. Except for brief quotations in critical publications or reviews, no part of this book may be reproduced in any manner without prior written permission from the publisher. Write: Permissions, Wipf and Stock Publishers, 199 W. 8th Ave., Suite 3, Eugene, OR 97401.

Pickwick Publications
An Imprint of Wipf and Stock Publishers
199 W. 8th Ave., Suite 3
Eugene, OR 97401

New Revised Standard Version Bible, copyright 1989, Division of Christian Education of the National Council of the Churches of Christ in the United States of America. Used by permission. All rights reserved.
www.wipfandstock.com

ISBN 13: 978-1-61097-994-8

Cataloging-in-Publication data:

Nessan, Craig L.

    The vitality of liberation theology / Craig L. Nessan ; foreword by Paul S. Chung.

    xvi + 158 p. ; cm. — Includes bibliographical references and indexes.

    Missional Church, Public Theology, World Christianity 3

    ISBN 13: 978-1-61097-994-8

    1. Liberation theology. 2. Theology, Doctrinal—Latin America—History—20th century. I. Chung, Paul S., 1958-. II. Series. III. Title.

BT83.57 .N47 2012

Manufactured in the U.S.A.

I dedicate this book to those friends who have most significantly accompanied me from the time this theme first emerged as a call that would not leave me alone to this day: James and Johanna Erdman, Chellaian and Malar Lawrence, Georg Kraus, Renate Wind, Beate Hofmann, Paul Chung, and Ulrich Duchrow. May God grant each of us such *compañeros en la lucha*!

And Mary said:

"My soul magnifies the Lord,
and my Spirit rejoices in God my Savior,
for he has looked with favor on the lowliness of his servant.
Surely, from now on all generations will call me blessed;
for the Mighty One has done great things for me, and holy is God's name.
His mercy is for those who fear him from generation to generation.
He has shown strength with his arm;
He has scattered the proud in the thoughts of their hearts.
He has brought down the powerful from their thrones,
and lifted up the lowly;
he has filled the hungry with good things,
and sent the rich away empty.
He has helped his servant Israel, in remembrance of his mercy,
according to the promise he made to his ancestors,
to Abraham and his descendants forever."

Luke 1:46–55

Contents

Foreword by Paul S. Chung / ix

Introduction / xiii

1 Poverty: The Imperative of a Liberation Theology / 1

2 Latin American History: A Liberationist Perspective / 14

3 Emergence and Development of Liberation Theology / 29

4 Reading the Bible through Liberation Eyes: Justice Trajectory and the Gospel of Luke / 62

5 Praxis: The Method of Liberation Theology / 78

6 Basic Christian Communities: The Agent of Liberation Theology / 93

7 Two Questions: Marxism and Violence? / 105

8 Dynamics of Polarization: North American Critics versus Liberation Theology / 124

9 How Social Is the Gospel? / 133

Conclusion: The Vitality of Liberation Theology / 146

Bibliography / 151

Name Index / 155

Subject Index / 157

Foreword

THIS FOREWORD IS FOR me a way of expressing gratitude, accompaniment, and solidarity. In *The Vitality of Liberation Theology*, Craig L. Nessan undertakes an impressive and thought-provoking attempt to chart, introduce, and clarify the genesis, development, setback, and future pertaining to several substantial issues in liberation theology in Latin America. He reflects on the subject of poverty as the point of departure for liberation theology, examining the background and scope of Latin American history, while analyzing the emergence and development of liberation theology in its initial stages. Furthermore, relating biblical perspective on oppressed people, Nessan gives an account of the methodological distinctiveness of social praxis as the critical epistemology underlying liberation theology. Social activism and the praxis of transformation are grounded in an ecclesiology of the poor that comes to expression in base Christian communities. A prophetic *diakonia* to the marginalized and the destitute is essential in missional ecclesiology and public theology.

Nessan's book is not a mere introduction of liberation theology. Instead, it entails a critical-constructive proposal concerning the consequences of justification by grace, freedom, and liberation. The author engages the critiques of North American scholars concerning the limitations of liberation theology, for instance, in relation to the controversial concept of Marxist social theory and the issue of violence. Nessan's clarification of the liberationist's selective reception of historical materialism is lucid rather than apologetic, because such a social theory serves as a sociohistorical, analytical tool in the interpretation of human life in the social political realm. As Nessan contends, several controversial tenets of Marxism (for instance, dialectical materialism as a comprehensive worldview, atheism, and materialistic reductionism among others) are fundamentally refused in the circle of liberation theology. Dependency theory, which liberation theology utilizes in connection with socioeconomic inquiry, contradicts the Marxist theory of political economy and its unilateral Eurocentric view of historical materialism.

Nonetheless, liberationists do not intend to discard Marx's own prophetic humanism, his critique of capitalism as a quasi-religion of mammon, and its critique of Christendom. Instead, they utilize Marx's humanist insight as self-critical *metanoia* to improve on the limitations of Christian religion, which has long been distorted in its wedding of crown and altar. Concerning the issues of institutionalized violence and counter-violence, Nessan's heart sides with Mahatma Gandhi and Martin Luther King Jr.

Social sinfulness has been brought to the theological agenda by the claims of liberation theology as a retrieval of the social dimension of healing in light of the gospel of Jesus Christ. However, the liberationist notion of the gospel has been challenged by several scholars in North America for reducing both the transcendental origin of the gospel and the eschatological fulfillment of the gospel to the political-immanentalist sphere. There is a warning about conflation of the gospel of God's kingdom and modernist-Marxist faith in progress. Regarding the debate and conflict of interpretations between liberation theology and its critics, Nessan's defense of the social dimension of the gospel, although modest, is deliberate and innovative.

Nessan investigates the scope and horizon of what liberation theology brings to the theological agenda concerning how necessarily social the gospel of Jesus Christ is, not merely in the quarter of liberation theology, but across the globe (including North America and Europe). According to this evaluation, liberation theology is the first major contribution originating from the Third World in the modern era. This refers to the significance of social topography for theological reflection in seeking to denounce the shackles of poverty and oppressive social structures of the neocolonial realities, ensuing in the aftermath of colonialism. Faith seeks understanding by taking issue with the status quo—those factors that condition, refract, and even distort human existence in its social location.

Even more, Nessan redirects attention toward the re-articulation of the social political dimension of the kingdom of God through a retrieval of the usable legacy of Western theology. The prophetic dimension of the gospel is not merely confined to the theological parlance of liberation theology, but its history is grounded in the biblical context and the Reformation theology of grace, threading its way into the work of

Foreword

North American and European theologians, notably in the theology of social gospel of Walter Rauschenbush, the Lutheran categories of Gustaf Wingren and Walter Altmann, the process categories of Schubert Ogden, and prophetically in the case of Karl Barth. Nessan's creative reading of Karl Barth's political theology with its gospel-law dynamism finds its echo in the Lutheran prophetic notion of *paranesis* (as the line and trajectory of the gospel) and Bonhoeffer's theology of *status confessionis* and his law-gospel hermeneutics from below. This perspective can nourish a discussion of God's mission, public theology, and World Christianity in the direction of public responsibility for social justice, shalom, and respect for the other.

Nessan's hermeneutical recovery of the meaning of the social critical horizon of the gospel acts as catalyst for penetrating between the Reformation theology of grace and liberation theology in a dynamic fusion of horizons. The Reformation teaching of justification by grace through faith insists upon the fact that *ecclesia semper reformanda* in light of the gospel means *viva vox evangelii*. This gospel-aspect does not tolerate injustice, notably in the economic sphere. Other than theologians, it was Karl Marx who already discerned the prophetic voice of the Reformer in questioning the Christian character of capital accumulation in relation to colonialism. A theology of grace is to be lived out in the praxis of discipleship, so that *societas et humanitas semper reformanda* for prophetic *diakonia* to those vulnerable and fragile—God's *massa perditionis*, the *minjung*-subaltern.

As Nessan knows, the Lutheran theology of law and gospel is neither non-political nor quietistic, but it entails the prophetic dimension of ideology critique. Liberation theology can find a coherent theological interlocutor in the Lutheran concepts of justification by grace and economic justice, *theologia crucis* and God's universal saving mission through two kingdoms (strategies!) embedded in three irreducible mandates. "Luther and Liberation" are not in binary opposition! This Lutheran synthesis has been contextualized notably in the circle of postcolonial *minjung* theology in East Asia and also in North America. Nessan is aware of critical comments about the "demise of liberation theology." Nonetheless, insofar as the gospel of Jesus Christ is life-giving, driven by forgiveness, freedom, and emancipation in the spirit of the God of Israel, the central claims of liberation theology continue to bring vitality and challenge to theological discourse and action. I find such a vision, fueled by the prophetic mission of Bartolomé de Las Casas in the period of Spanish conquest, stimulating for the study of Missional Church, Public Theology, and World Christianity. Liberation theology as critical reflection on Christian praxis in light of the Word of God is not in demise, but remains an impulse and dialogue partner for contemporary theological endeavors in articulating the prophetic dimension of the Word of God in different times and places for generations to come.

Paul S. Chung
Luther Seminary, St. Paul, Minnesota
Easter 2012

Introduction

LIBERATION THEOLOGY IRRUPTED LIKE a rocket in Latin American church and society in the 1960s. In the wake of the *aggiornamento* ("bringing up to date") of Vatican II, the Roman Catholic Church made a sharp turn toward engaging cultures and the harsh social realities suffered by millions of people throughout the world. The exciting new ecclesial climate created perfect conditions for unprecedented ecumenical cooperation, especially in addressing urgent issues of poverty and oppression under which vast numbers of hungry and unprivileged people dwelled.

Amid the forces for radical social change—epitomized by the witness of worker-priests in France, Martin Luther King Jr. and Thomas Merton in the United States, and Che Guevara and Camilo Torres in Latin America—both Roman Catholics and Protestants rediscovered the biblical witness to justice for the poor and tested available tools of social analysis to answer the question, "Why?" Mobilized by bishops, priests, and pastors, a people's movement began to arise from the *barrio* dwellers and *campesinos* throughout Latin America.

The magnitude of the pressure for structural change soon ignited formidable resistance, both among the elite economic classes and reactionary segments of the churches. In the Roman Catholic Church, those seeking to repeal the innovations of Vatican II—and in the Protestant churches, the growing tide of US exported Evangelicalism and Pentecostalism—challenged the core convictions of liberation theology. Even more, the use of Marxist social analysis and the threat of Christians engaging in revolutionary violence as a means of social change led to organized efforts to neutralize the influence of the progressive bishops, priests, pastors, theologians, and people formed by liberation theology.

The story of the emergence and proliferation of liberation theology, as well as the opposition to this movement both within and without Latin America, is one of the most significant developments in Christianity in the last third of the twentieth century. What we today call World Christianity in many ways found its first potent voice crying out from Latin

America. This book introduces the signal importance of Latin American liberation theology to a new generation in a new century, for whom this story is lesser known.

Chapter 1 introduces the theme of poverty as the starting point for the theological reflection and call to action which is liberation theology. Chapter 2 views the scope of Latin American history through the perspective of liberation theology, and chapter 3 analyzes the emergence and development of liberation theology in its first decades. Chapter 4 reflects on the discovery by liberation theologians of the Bible's liberation trajectory, good news for the poor, and demonstrates how the biblical message functions as social dynamite for oppressed people. Chapter 5 explains "praxis" as the very method of liberation theology and explains the elements of this distinctive method.

Chapter 6 describes how the ministries of countless base Christian communities, made up of the poor, served as the primary agents of the kind of social activism and transformation generated by liberation theology. Chapter 7 confronts two of the most challenging questions raised against liberation theology: its use of Marxist social analysis and the sometime advocacy of violence as a means of social change by liberation theologians. Chapter 8 dissects the polarization of views generated by liberation theology, particularly in the North American context—for and against. Chapter 9 evaluates the contributions of liberation theology by posing the critical question, how social is the Gospel of Jesus Christ? The conclusion traces the impact of Latin American liberation theology on all subsequent theological discourse across the globe, including North America and Europe.

Latin American liberation theology is the *first* major theological movement to have its origin in the Third World in the modern period. This elevates it to monumental significance for the entire history of theology. The social location for theological reflection could no longer be confined to the university, divinity school, or seminary in Europe or North America. Instead, the social location for the "doing" of theology shifted dramatically to the communities of the poor, those seeking to cast off the shackles of poverty and oppressive social structures.

At the exact same time in North America, catalyzed by the prophetic writings and teaching of James Cone, black liberation theology emerged as the voice for liberation among those suffering from the legacy of slavery and racism. Soon, "contextual" theologies, advocating social equality and economic justice, emerged across the continents, wherever Christian people began to read the Bible through liberation lenses: Anti-apartheid theology in South Africa and Namibia, *Minjung* theology in Korea, *Dalit* theology in India, and Palestinian liberation theology. *Kairos* processes issued prophetic challenges to the status quo that allowed millions of people to suffer without voice and without the most basic provisions needed for survival. The dawn of Latin American liberation theology inaugurated a new era in the global theological landscape.

I want to express my gratitude to many partners, colleagues, and friends who have accompanied me on the theological journey that began with my earliest engagement with liberation theology. This book is dedicated to them. My deep thanks are extended to those editors who have granted permission to rework material from their publications into a new and expanded form in this book: *Currents in Theology and Mission*, *Dialog: A Journal of Theology*, Scholars Press, and Fortress Press. Sincere gratitude is also due Andrew Dietzel and Deborah Cote, my student assistants, for excellent comments, proofreading, and help with the bibliography.

Craig L. Nessan
Wartburg Theological Seminary, Dubuque, Iowa, USA
Pentecost 2012

1

Poverty

The Imperative of a Liberation Theology

"Blessed are you poor, for yours is the kingdom of God"
—Luke 6:20

IVAN PETRELLA HAS ARGUED that after taking a long and necessary route through the use of multiple forms of social analysis—culture, race, gender, heterosexism, etc.—liberation theology needs to return with focus to its original ethical impulse: economic analysis of the causes of poverty and praxis to address massive and growing poverty.[1] Since the emergence of Latin America liberation theology in the late 1960s, considerable thought has been devoted to the meaning of this and the many other passages of Scripture which speak of the poor. This chapter demonstrates how the scandal of poverty gave rise to the imperative of a liberation theology, which seeks to mediate between the biblical witness and contemporary reality.

George V. Pixley characterized three positions which Christians commonly assume regarding the biblical meaning of poverty.[2] *First*, poverty can be *spiritualized*. Here "the Bible does not speak of material poverty, but rather of a lack of attachment to material goods and dependence rather upon God." *Second*, there exists a purely *material* view in which poverty is understood in an exclusively material sense and in which the poor will be "the bearers of the Kingdom which will end the current class society." *Third*, there is a *progressivist* view which emphasizes the perfor-

---

1. Cf. Petrella, *Beyond Liberation Theology: A Polemic* (London: SCM, 2008) 83–112.
2. For this and the following quotes, see George V. Pixley, "People of God: Popular Majorities in the Bible," *Foundations* 23 (1980) 368.

mance of good works and acts of charity in order to improve the lot of the poor. Pixley notes that such conflicting understandings of the biblical witness is a complex affair because each of these positions can be justified on the basis of particular biblical texts.

This conflict in understandings about the meaning of poverty in the Bible has been dealt with by several liberation theologians. Out of their reflections has emerged something of a consensus. Three steps are required in order to interpret adequately the biblical witness regarding poverty. These three steps are concisely summarized in the title of an article by José Míguez Bonino, "Poverty as Curse, Blessing and Challenge."[3] Although different terminology has been used by other liberation theologians to describe these elements, their conclusions have been strikingly similar.

POVERTY AS CURSE, BLESSING, AND CHALLENGE

The *first step* in interpreting the biblical witness regarding poverty is the recognition that the dominant biblical judgment is that poverty is a "curse" (Míguez Bonino). Others have described this aspect of the biblical witness by calling poverty "a scandalous condition" (Gutiérrez)[4] or simply "evil" (Barreiro).[5] In this first step, a massive trajectory of biblical texts can be cited—from the Mosaic law, the prophets, Job, the teachings of Jesus, and the New Testament epistles—all of which testify to the biblical fact that poverty "is a scandalous condition inimical to human dignity and therefore contrary to the will of God."[6] Poverty is a wretched condition which is a scandal to God and is to be rejected by humanity. Moreover, poverty is not a condition which occurs by chance but instead is the result of human injustice and thereby is to be condemned, as happens throughout the prophetic writings.[7] Even more than mere condemnation, there is the prominent biblical demand that those in authority take "positive

---

3. José Míguez Bonino, "Poverty as Curse, Blessing and Challenge," *Iliff Review* 34 (1977) 3–13.

4. Gustavo Gutiérrez, *A Theology of Liberation: History, Politics, and Salvation*, trans. and ed. Caridad Inda and John Eagleson (Maryknoll, NY: Orbis, 1973) 291–96.

5. Alvaro Barreiro, "Grass-Roots Ecclesial Communities and the Evangelization of the Poor," *Foundations* 23 (1980) 314–16.

6. Gutiérrez, *A Theology of Liberation*, 291.

7. For biblical references regarding the prophetic condemnation of the abuses which cause poverty, see Gutiérrez, *Theology of Liberation*, 293.

and concrete measures to prevent poverty" in order to correct situations of injustices.[8]

When the theologians of liberation speak about poverty as a "blessing" as a *second step* in understanding the biblical witness, they most certainly do not mean that "poverty is the most certain road to eternal felicity."[9] Physical poverty is not to be embraced because it leads to eventual rewards in the afterlife. Rather, physical poverty is an affront to God's justice. When the Bible speaks of poverty as a "blessing," an "ideal," or as "spiritual childhood," something dramatically different is intended. Gutiérrez negates the blessing of poverty with reference to many prophetic and New Testament texts, especially the Matthean and Lukan versions of the Sermon on the Mount/Plain. The possible blessing of poverty only makes sense insofar as the poor are understood as those who are free of material obstacles which limit their ability to be open to God. This is what Gutiérrez means by "spiritual childhood"—not the poverty of physical want, but spiritual poverty in which one can be open to listen for God's voice. Barreiro, with a slightly different emphasis, speaks of poverty as an "ideal," which allows the individual, freed from material encumbrances, to become more able to love. Poverty allows one to become more compassionate to those who are in need. Exemplary for Barreiro is the poverty of the church in Acts which was not the result of striving to approximate an abstract ideal but instead the natural outgrowth of a life lived for the sake of others.[10]

Gutiérrez furthermore affirms that the poor are blessed because in Christ the kingdom of God has already begun. In Christ God has taken the side of the poor and through the Christ event comes blessing. In Christ the forces of justice have been released which will ultimately lead to the elimination of physical poverty.[11] Therefore, the poor are blessed wherever the kingdom of God becomes manifest. Similarly, Míguez Bonino emphasizes that in the coming of Christ, God's good news to the poor is already coming true. Jesus reverses the present order of things.

---

8. Ibid., 293–94.

9. Archbishop Pedro Pascual Farfan as quoted by John William Hart, "Topia and Utopia in Colombia and Peru: The Theory and Practice of Camilo Torres and Gustavo Gutiérrez in Their Hisotrical Contexts" (PhD diss., Union Theological Seminary, 1978) 184.

10. Barreiro, "Grass-Roots Ecclesial Communities," 315–16.

11. Gutiérrez, *Theology of Liberation*, 298.

Kings are dethroned and deposed and the hungry are raised up and filled with good things (Luke 2:52–53). The poor are privileged recipients of the gospel. In fact, the poor have an *epistemological privilege* in apprehending this gospel. As the poor claim the gospel for themselves in their poverty, they receive God's blessing and begin to live in the power of the kingdom by which physical poverty will be overcome.[12]

The *third step* in interpreting the biblical witness regarding poverty views poverty as a *challenge* (Míguez Bonino) which yet remains to be overcome. Other liberation theologians speak of "a commitment to liberation" (Barreiro) and "solidarity and protest" (Gutiérrez). Not only is poverty a scandalous condition contrary to God's intention and a spiritual blessing by which God's kingdom comes to the poor, but poverty is also a challenge which demands a change in the present economic order. The biblical witness points toward "a transformation of the conditions of our life, by the creation of a new world and a new day for all mankind."[13] Poverty challenges those who are not poor to join in the struggle of the poor and be transformed by the personal encounter with them. Poverty as a moral challenge means choosing to participate in the sufferings of the poor in the struggle to bring about the construction of a more just society. Gutiérrez writes that Christian poverty is "solidarity with the poor and is a protest against poverty."[14] He points to the example of the early church as depicted in Acts as a church of solidarity and protest. Solidarity with those in poverty means choosing to be poor not in an attempt to idealize poverty but in order to issue a *protest* against it and to struggle to *abolish* it.

Enrique Dussel has described the dialectical relationship in the New Testament between the kingdom of God as "already" inaugurated and as "not yet" fulfilled, especially as it applies to the overcoming of material poverty.[15] Whereas many contemporary theologians have emphasized the future character of God's kingdom and minimized its significance for the present, the theology of liberation (like the earlier Social Gospel) stresses the implications of the kingdom of God for the present struggle against poverty, yet without claiming that the kingdom can be achieved by mere

---

12. Míguez Bonino, "Poverty as Curse, Blessing and Challenge," 10.

13. Ibid., 11.

14. Gutiérrez, *Theology of Liberation*, 300–301.

15. Enrique Dussel, "The Kingdom of God and the Poor," *International Review of Mission* 68 (1979) 115–30.

human effort.[16] Especially relevant for the theologians of liberation are those biblical texts which point toward a systemic understanding of the causes of poverty. Moreover, special significance has been given to those passages that encourage the church to lend solidarity to the poor as their own agents in overcoming poverty and oppression.

The theologians of liberation affirm *the role of the church* in serving the poor as they become active participants in the struggle against poverty. Ellacuría argued that the Latin American Church must claim its primary charisma by becoming the "church of the poor."[17] Barriero declared that the church must announce liberation to the poor in order to remain faithful to "the mission of Jesus, the Messiah of the poor."[18] Gutiérrez spoke of solidarity with the poor and protest against poverty by the church as "a much-needed sign of the authenticity of its mission."[19] Míguez Bonino meanwhile asserted that the Church needs to "discern the signs of the times" by becoming transformed by the witness of the poor in their struggle against poverty.[20]

The theology of liberation by no means understands the relationship between the church and the poor as a one-way street. There is a deep awareness of the need for the poor to evangelize the church. Dussel, for example, has written prophetically that "the authentic epiphany of the Word of God is that word spoken by the poor majority who says, 'I am hungry.'"[21] Liberation theologians claim that the poor reveal the presence of Christ to the church in a way which demands recognition.[22] The poor remind the church of who Jesus Christ is and where he chooses to reveal himself in the world today. The poor are not mere objects of

---

16. Cf. Leonardo Boff, *Church: Charism and Power: Liberation Theology and the Institutional Church*, trans. John W. Diercksmeier (London: SCM, 1985) 10.

17. Ignacio Ellacuría, *Freedom Made Flesh: The Mission of Christ and His Church*, trans. John Drury (Maryknoll, NY: Orbis, 1976) 146.

18. Barreiro, "Grass-Roots Ecclesial Communities," 316.

19. Gutiérrez, *Theology of Liberation*, 302.

20. Míguez Bonino, "Poverty as Curse, Blessing and Challenge," 12.

21. Enrique Dussel, *A History of the Church in Latin America: Colonialism to Liberation (1492–1979)*, trans. Alan Neely (Grand Rapids: Eerdmans, 1981) 16. Cf. also 305.

22. Gustavo Gutiérrez, "The Irruption of the Poor in Latin America and the Christian Communities of the Common People," in *The Challenge of Basic Christian Communities*, ed. Sergio Torres and John Eagleson, trans. John Drury (Maryknoll, NY: Orbis, 1981) 120. The work of Gutiérrez insists on the centrality of the poor as the revealers of Christ and the gospel. Cf. Gutiérrez, *The Power of the Poor in History*, trans. Robert R. Barr (Maryknoll, NY: Orbis, 1983) 21–22, 52–53, 105, 150, and 214.

Christian charity. Instead they reveal the identity of Christ in a profound way. Matthew 25:31–46, the parable of the last judgment, has played a major role in shaping the consciousness of the theology of liberation in this regard. The poor serve as a sacrament of Christ's presence in the contemporary world. As we do it to the least of these—the hungry, thirsty, sick, and imprisoned ones—we do it to Christ himself.

Liberation theology witnesses to the living legacy of the biblical word as it relates to the contemporary situation of extreme poverty in Latin America and across the globe. A dynamic hermeneutical circle is enacted as biblical texts inform the contemporary reality of poverty and the contemporary reality of poverty poses new questions to the biblical texts. The biblical witness speaks a prophetic word to the church about its mission in the face of a continent and world overwhelmed by extreme poverty. The churches of the North thereby are challenged to new commitment and active engagement on behalf of the poor both at home and across continents.

THE DIMENSIONS OF POVERTY IN LATIN AMERICA

There are a variety of complex and interconnected factors that combine to constitute the reality of poverty in Latin America.

> Lack of industries, unemployment, illiteracy, disease, lack of skilled labor and low salaries, lack of roads, obsolete techniques of agriculture, the transformation of vast areas for cattle-raising, and other questions show a pretty complex reality.[23]

When one begins to examine these interwoven factors and the linkages between them, it becomes difficult to establish cause and effect relations. Across Latin America and the Caribbean 534 million people live in poverty, according to recent World Bank statistics. Fifty-seven million people on this continent live on less than $1 per day and 132 million people on less than $2 per day. This section offers a description of several key factors contributing to Latin American poverty. They are here formally distinguished from one another in order to give clearer picture of the reality of poverty. By naming the following factors, we intend to make the reality of poverty more concrete. No claim is made to be exhaustive. In any case, one must remain mindful of the interrelationship and dependence of

---

23. Dom Moacyr as quoted by Alvaro Barreiro, "Grass-Roots Ecclesial Communities," 298.

these factors upon one another. These are some of the basic themes which recur in the literature of liberation theology.

Malnutrition

Poverty is often equated with hunger or malnutrition. It is perhaps the most visible and shocking manifestation of poverty. Numerous studies are available depicting in detail the extent to which hunger and malnutrition stalk the planet and the human toll which is paid.[24] Statistics tell one story:

> The LAC poverty rate (measured according to the standard of under $2 a day) averaged about 25% in 2005, with individual country rates ranging from 4% in Uruguay to 47% in Nicaragua.... Falling in the middle is the "Southern Cone" region of Argentina, Bolivia, Brazil, Chile, Paraguay, and Uruguay, which averaged 18.8%; Central America and Mexico averaged 29.2%; and the region of the Andean Mountains averaged 31.4%.... The rates measuring against the poverty lines of individual countries yield a somewhat different picture. In Honduras, for example, 72% of the population in 2005 lived below the country's poverty line, while 36% lived on less than $2 a day. In Chile 5% of the population lived on less than $2 a day, but 19% lived below the country's poverty line. By contrast, in Jamaica about 22% of people lived below the country's poverty line, but 43% made less than $2 a day. In El Salvador the numbers were nearly the same, 39% and 41%, respectively.[25]

Comparable statistics could be cited for other Latin American countries.

Even more graphic and disturbing is the following description of the process of starvation in which statistics begin to take on human form:

> The victim of starvation burns up his own body fats, muscles and tissues for fuel. His body quite literally consumes itself and deteriorates rapidly. The kidneys, liver and endocrine system soon cease to function properly. A shortage of carbohydrates, which play a vital role in brain chemistry, affects the mind. Lassitude and confusion set in, so that starvation victims often seem unaware of

---

24. For a recent collection of global poverty statistics, see http://www.globalissues.org/article/26/poverty-facts-and-stats, October 9, 2010.

25. "Poverty and the Developing World—Latin America and the Caribbean," http://www.libraryindex.com/pages/2676/Poverty-in-Developing-World-LATIN-AMERICA-CARIBBEAN.html, October 9, 2010.

their plight. The body's defenses drop; disease kills most famine victims before they have time to starve to death.[26]

Such is the process of starvation by which millions of human beings in Latin America suffer to various degrees.

Disease

Immunity to disease is significantly diminished as a result of malnutrition. Diarrhea, parasitic infestations, and measles are among those diseases to which the malnourished poor are most vulnerable. The unavailability of adequate health care, immunization, and medications complicates and magnifies the effects of disease on a malnourished population. Especially vulnerable to disease are infants and young children. When analyzing poverty statistics, it is difficult to distinguish between those who die of hunger and those who die from opportunistic diseases whose onset was given occasion by malnutrition.

Infant Mortality

Although infant mortality in Latin America has improved in recent decades, the discrepancy between the developed and developing world remains shocking: "Of the annual average 10 million child deaths under the age of five, 97% occur in the developing world of avoidable causes—this equals the entire child population of France or Italy. Each year 2.2 million children die for lack of immunization and 15 million children have been orphaned due to HIV/AIDS, equalling the total population of Germany or the United Kingdom."[27] Across all of Latin America there has been uneven progress:

> In Latin America and the Caribbean the infant mortality rate has declined dramatically to 35 per 1,000 live births from 59 per 1,000 in the early 1980s. Bolivia and Haiti have more than halved their infant mortality rates since the 1950s. Infant mortality is defined as deaths among children under 1 year of age. . . . The report warns, however, that the extent and speed of these improvements were not equal for all countries or for all groups within individual countries. "Inequities persisted and, in some cases, grew."[28]

26. *Time* (Nov. 11, 1975) 68, as quoted by Jose Miguez Bonino, "Poverty as Curse, Blessing and Challenge," *Iliff Review* 34 (Fall 1977) 6.

27. Petrella, *Beyond Liberation Theology*, 42.

28. Pan American Health Organization, "Inequalities in Infant Mortality in the

Poverty

The malnutrition of the mother during pregnancy is a major factor in infant mortality. Wherever breastfeeding gives way to the use of infant formula, there are significant implications for the poor in terms of cost, hygiene, nutrition, and loss of immunological protection, which has contributed to the incidence of infant mortality. Undernourished infants are also especially susceptible to fatal disease, a problem compounded by a shortage of medical facilities and medications.

> In spite of these problems, progress in overcoming infant mortality has been achieved at relatively low cost and with immediate results with the introduction of a fourfold program to combat it. The four techniques advocated by the United Nations Children's Fund have included oral rehydration therapy, growth monitoring, expanded immunization, and education about the advantages of breast feeding and supplementary nutrition.[29]

Land Distribution

A factor of major significance is the unequal distribution of land in Latin America. Leopoldo Zea has called this "the central problem of the Americas."[30] According to Zea, redistribution of land ownership is the key to economic and social transformation. The uneven distribution of land in Latin America has its origins in the colonial period following the Iberian conquest (see chapter 2). The baronial style of life in which a minority controlled an inordinate share of the land has survived through the centuries and evolved into ever new forms. Today it is often corporations which possess an inordinate share of the land.

> A major cause of the dramatic inequities in income in Latin America is the region's history of land distribution. The World Bank's Office of Land Policy and Administration reports that Latin America's forty million indigenous peoples have not historically been given land rights because government priority has always leaned toward allowing for the greatest—usually corporate or business-oriented—use of natural resources. In *Models for Recognizing Indigenous Land Rights in Latin America* (World Bank,

---

American Region: Basic Elements for Analysis." Online: http://www.paho.org/english/sha/be_v22n2-inequalitiesIM.htm, May 22, 2012.

29. See James P. Grant, "The State of the World's Children," published by the United Nations Children's Fund, 1–26.

30. See Leopoldo Zea, *Latin America and the World*, trans. Frances K. Hendricks and Beatrice Berler (Norman: University of Oklahoma Press, 1969) 33–51.

October 2004), Roque Roldán Ortiga reports that historically, Latin America's indigenous land rights system was essential for the livelihoods, culture, inheritance patterns, and basic survival of the native people.[31]

Furthermore, the food policies of the developed world favor large corporate farming in the developed world at the expense of small farmers in the developing world.[32] These endemic policies are always exacerbated by natural disasters, such as drought or devastating earthquakes.[33] Jon Sobrino writes of the situation in El Salvador, an especially egregious example of inequitable land distribution, where the gap between the haves and have nots are revealed for all to see in the wake of a natural disaster, such as an earthquake.[34] Such disparity in land distribution and ownership was one of the chief causes of the civil war that broke out in El Salvador in the 1980s. Even in countries such as Mexico, where the inequities are less dramatic and where land reform has been dictated by law, wealthy landowners have been able to employ political influence to thwart enforcement of these laws in order to maintain their advantages.

Export Cropping

Related to the problem of land distribution is the challenging problem of land usage. "Export cropping" refers to the phenomenon by which, instead of being used to grow food staples for an impoverished population, land is used to grow export crops such as coffee, cotton, bananas, sugar, or beef that are exported to foreign markets. Traditionally, in Central America roughly half of the cultivated land, and generally the most fertile land, has been used for such export crops.

Such a system might be justifiable were the income from such export crops used to care for the needs of the poor people who live in these countries. Unfortunately, that is seldom the case and relatively few actually profit from the export crop system. Often the Latin American people are

---

31. "Poverty and the Developing World—Latin America and the Caribbean," http://www.libraryindex.com/pages/2676/Poverty-in-Developing-World-LATIN-AMERICA-CARIBBEAN.html, October 9, 2010.

32. Roger Thurow and Scott Kilman, *Enough: Why the World's Poorest Starve in an Age of Plenty* (New York: PublicAffairs, 2009) 85–97.

33. Michael Elliott, Jeffrey Kluger, and Richard Lacayo, eds., *Earthquake Haiti: Tragedy and Hope* (New York: Time, 2010).

34. Jon Sobrino, *Where Is God? Earthquake, Terrorism, Barbarity, and Hope* (Maryknoll, NY: Orbis, 2004) 67–70.

forced to pay higher prices for food which is subsequently imported from other countries rather than using the land of their own country to grow their own food.

A related problem involves the foreign export of natural resources. Precious natural resources, such as minerals and oil, have been exported to aid the industrial development of other countries, a process in which relatively few have reaped the financial gain and the vast majority gained nothing. The depletion of natural resources degrades the environment, further retards the economy, and minimizes the possibility of future economic growth. The land, depleted of natural resources, is yet poorer.

Environmental Degradation

One inevitable consequence of extreme poverty is the degradation of the environment. First, the legal systems of Latin American countries often fail to enact environmental protections out of a deference to the interests of international business. Second, those who are poor are pressed to satisfy their most urgent need for survival at the expense of care for the environment.

> If Latin America and the Caribbean continue on the path to market liberalization without changes in values or structural transformations, by 2032 the environment will be in deep crisis, warns a broad investigation sponsored by UNEP [United Nations Environmental Program]. . . . The inhabitants of the region lose as many as 11 years off their lives due to causes related to environmental degradation. . . . In the past 30 years, environmental deterioration has worsened, evident in critical areas such as loss of forests and biodiversity, degradation of soil and water supplies, urban pollution, and the effect of all this on the health of the region's population, says the report.[35]

The problem of environmental degradation is one that liberation theology was slow to address, but it has attained growing urgency in recent decades.[36]

---

35. Tierramerica webpage, http://www.tierramerica.net/2004/0301/iarticulo.shtml, October 9, 2010.

36. One early voice among liberation theologians advocating care for the earth was Leonardo Boff, *Cry of the Earth, Cry of the Poor*, trans. Phillip Berryman (Maryknoll, NY: Orbis, 1997).

The Vitality of Liberation Theology

Inadequate Structures

> Increasingly in the last three decades, the "privatization" of goods, services, and knowledge previously considered public has emerged as a defining characteristic of the cultural, political, and economic ethos. Privatization in the current era gives to companies or individuals, often not accountable to the communities impacted, ownership of basic goods; of services such as water, electricity, health care, and education; and of intellectual property in the form of patents. . . . This trend spans the globe and has far-reaching and profound moral implications.[37]

Undernutrition of millions is rarely the result of inadequate food supplies. Instead, poverty results from inadequate structures—the ways governments and corporations manage global business and trade. Hunger persists because the reality of poor people does not affect political or economic "success." Governments—Latin American and foreign, in cooperation with international corporations—preserve vested economic and political interests by legalizing trade agreements which result in social structures inadequate in addressing their most basic human needs. The reality of poverty in Latin America is sustained by political and economic systems which function to preserve benefits for elites at the expense of those at the bottom of the socioeconomic ladder.

In the late twentieth century, the form of government in Latin America most effective at maintaining the status quo for the privileged few was the military regime. Even with the more recent trend toward elected democracies, governments in league with corporations and banking interests privilege the wealthy at the expense of the poor. Corporate interests, especially those of foreign concerns, have been favored by the governments, legal system, and judiciary in most Latin American countries. Thereby the traditional disparity of wealth has been maintained. Dissent has been stifled, often violently.[38]

The ways in which governments exercise power in the repression of political dissent has been capably monitored by the work of Amnesty

---

37. Cynthia D. Moe-Lobeda, *Public Church: For the Life of the World* (Minneapolis: Augsburg Fortress, 2004) 9–10.

38. For a graphic description of the social, economic, political, military, and religious factors in late-twentieth century Latin American history, see Penny Lernoux, *Cry of the People* (New York: Penguin, 1982). Lernoux documents numerous cases of persecution against those who have sought reform, especially those within the church.

Poverty

International.[39] The 2010 report of Amnesty International, for example, documents the instances of political power in Latin America to suppress dissent. Violations can be cited for each Latin American country.

It is the structural dimensions of poverty in Latin America that the theology of liberation has attempted to address most directly. Structural injustice is understood as the fundamental cause of poverty in Latin America. Liberation theology finds inadequate those paradigms which explain the problems of Latin America according to "underdevelopment," a situation which could be gradually overcome through a process of development. Rather, the theology of liberation operates according to an alternative theoretical model, that of dependency theory, to explain the structural nature of Latin American poverty. The theory of dependency, together with the biblical themes of justice and liberation, serves as an essential presupposition of liberation theology.

SUMMARY

We have examined some of the basic factors contributing to the existence of poverty in Latin America. These are by no means comprehensive. To these, many other factors could be added and documented in greater detail:

> The socio-economic, political, and cultural situation of the peoples of Latin America poses a challenge to our Christian conscience. Unemployment, malnutrition, alcoholism, infant mortality, illiteracy, prostitution, ever growing inequality between rich and poor, racial and educational discrimination, exploitation, and so forth: these are the factors that go to make up a situation of institutionalized violence in Latin America.[40]

This testimony helpfully directs attention to the manifestations of poverty as they might be viewed from a pastoral perspective. Poverty, in all its human dimensions, is the urgent imperative for the engagement of liberation theology.

---

39. *Amnesty International Report 2010—A Survey of Amnesty International's Work on Political Imprisonment, Torture, and Executions* (London: Amnesty International, 2010). See the section on "The Americas." Online: http://thereport.amnesty.org/regions/americas, October 9, 2010.

40. "Final Document of the Convention," from the First Convention of Christians for Socialism, held in Santiago, Chile, April 1972, in *Christians and Socialism*, ed. Eagleson, 163.

2

Latin American History

A Liberationist Perspective

LATIN AMERICAN LIBERATION THEOLOGY, which is so closely bound to praxis, lives in a vital connection to the history in which it developed. Its rise has been accompanied by a surge of interest in the history of Latin America,[1] with emphasis both upon the history of the Latin American church[2] and recent events which have stimulated and marked the growth of liberation thought.[3] This chapter examines the significant factors which have shaped liberation theology's understanding of history. This includes its view both of Latin America's more distant past as well as its reading of current events.

---

1. For a brief overview of current research into Latin American history, see Hans-Jürgen Prien, "Einleitung," in *Lateinamerika: Gesellschaft, Kirche, Theologie*, ed. Hans-Jürgen Prien (Göttingen: Vandenhoeck & Ruprecht, 1981) 1:1–14.

2. Two major historical works which describe the history of the church in Latin America are Hans-Jürgen Prien, *Die Geschichte des Christentums in Lateinamerika* (Göttingen: Vandenhoeck & Ruprecht, 1978) and Enrique Dussel, *A History of the Church in Latin America: Colonialism to Liberation*, trans. Alan Neely (Grand Rapids: Eerdmans, 1981). Enrique Dussel, *History and the Theology of Liberation*, trans. John Drury (Maryknoll, NY: Orbis, 1976) includes six lectures by Dussel, which provide an overview of Latin American history as it relates to the theology of liberation.

3. There are many contributions to an understanding of the relationship between historical events and liberation theology. Emphasizing the struggle for human rights, the role of the Roman Catholic Church, and US policy in Latin America is Penny Lernoux, *Cry of the People* (New York: Penguin, 1980). Important articles are also available in the two-volume work edited by Hans-Jürgen Prien, *Lateinamerika: Gesellschaft, Kirche, Theologie*. Volume 1 contains two articles of special importance: Othmar Noggler, "Das erste Entwicklungsjahrzehnt. Vom. II Vatikanischen Konzil bis Medellin," 19–70, and Enrique Dussel, "Die Lateinamerikanische Kirche von Medellin bis Puebla (1968–1979)," 71–113. Volume 2 contains Jose Comblin, "Theologie der Befreiung in Lateinamerika," 13–38.

Latin American History

Three preliminary remarks are in order. First, liberation theology's understanding of history is in many ways at variance with traditional readings. The primary reason for this is that liberation theology seeks to interpret history from the point of view of the victims of history whereas conventional approaches to history draw their normative interpretation from the victors. This makes liberation theology's understanding of history at times contentious and controversial. For the interpretation of recent events, perhaps only a historian separated by time will be able to offer a less partisan account. In the meantime, this history is being interpreted by those deeply involved in the very events described which inevitably colors interpretation.

Secondly, it is clear that a nuanced understanding of the historical dynamics influencing the theology of liberation requires consideration of the particular historical development of each of the individual Latin American countries. In a theology which so strongly emphasizes context, the particular context of each of the countries plays a significant role beyond the historical and cultural elements which they share in common.[4] Such an analysis of the individual countries, however, is beyond the scope of this chapter. Primary attention is given to the historical factors which have had a more general influence throughout Latin America.

Thirdly, it is essential to note that history is more than an accounting of the events which make newspaper headlines. For this reason it is of importance to underscore the significance of the formation of numerous (estimates once ranged up to 150,000) "base Christian communities" for Latin American history. The history of liberation theology and Latin America cannot be limited to those accounts limited to secular history or

---

4. The value of considering the historical particularities of each of the individual Latin American countries becomes clear when reading the contextual differences between Colombia and Peru in John William Hart, "Topia and Utopia in Colombia and Peru—The Theory and Practice of Camilo Torres and Gustavo Gutierrez in Their Historical Contexts," PhD diss. (New York: Union Theological Seminary, 1978). A brief survey arranged according to individual countries is provided in Enrique Dussel, "Current Events in Latin America (1972–1980)," in *The Challenge of Basic Christian Communities*, ed. Sergio Torres and John Eagleson, trans. John Drury (Maryknoll, NY: Orbis, 1981) 77–102, and Dussel, *A History of the Church in Latin America*, 148–76. For more detailed descriptions of Argentina and Brazil by Hans-Jürgen Prien, and of Chile and Cuba by Othmar Noggler, see Hans-Jürgen Prien, ed., *Lateinamerika: Gesellschaft, Kirche, Theologie*, 1:115–303. Dussel, *A History of the Church in Latin America*, 28, argues for the possibility of describing Latin America culture apart from a complete analysis of the individual countries.

to the history of the institutional church. Nor would it be adequate to examine the writings of the liberation theologians as an historical factor in isolation from the reality of the "grass-roots" church. To be sure, secular and official ecclesiastical events (as well as the books, articles, and unpublished manuscripts of the liberation theologians) have played a central role in this history. But even more the history of the theology of liberation has been written by the activity of the people, the poor, who have affirmed God's liberating presence in their midst. In many discussions of the significant historical factors shaping Latin American liberation theology, this vital dimension has been overlooked. The life of the base Christian communities needs to remain a constant reference point when describing history in relationship to liberation theology.[5]

This chapter describes the central events which recur in the literature of the theology of liberation and constitute its particular understanding of Latin American history, past and present. Because of the intimate and vital connection between liberation thought and the historical context in which it has arisen, liberation theology's understanding of history is in many ways constitutive of the theology itself.

COLONIAL CHRISTENDOM (1492–1808)

Prior to the conquest and colonizing of Latin America, there existed two major civilizations, the Inca and the Mayan-Aztec, as well as other native cultures, for example, the Chibchas in Colombia.[6] The Iberian "discoverers" of the "New World" did not enter upon a land which had no prior history but rather forcefully imposed their culture and will upon the native peoples. As John Hart writes: "The conquistadores had a twofold objective: The conversion of the indigenous peoples and the acquisition of their wealth."[7] The history of this period is marked by the "genocide

---

5. Indispensable for understanding the contribution of the basic Christian communities to liberation theology are Ernesto Cardenal, *The Gospel in Solentiname*, 4 vols., trans. Donald D. Walsh (Maryknoll, NY: Orbis, 1976-1982); Sergio Torres and John Eagleson, eds., *The Challenge of Basic Christian Communities*; and Alvaro Barreiro, *Basic Ecclesial Communities: The Evangelization of the Poor*, trans. Barbara Campbell (Maryknoll, NY: Orbis, 1982).

6. Enrique Dussel, *History and the Theology of Liberation,* 42, and Dussel, *A History of the Church in Latin America,* 37.

7. Hart, "Topia and Utopia in Colombia and Peru," 28. Dussel, *A History of the Church in Latin America,* 39 and 41-43, confirms this judgment, noting the inseparability of the evangelical and economic motives.

of native peoples" and "slavery and dependence upon the European metropoli," things which "have little in common with the harmless and therefore false notion that the white man colonized the rest of the world in order to spread civilization, religion, knowledge and development."[8] It is estimated that the native population was reduced from 100 million to 10-12 million in less than a century after the Spanish conquest.[9] The culture of the native people was likewise decimated, submerged beneath that of their conquerors. The church was an accomplice in this sordid history, the religious rationale for the colonization process in which the Catholic faith was imposed upon the native people as an indistinguishable dimension of Spanish rule.[10]

> The salvation of these infidels through their incorporation into the Church was the recognized motive for Spain's work in America.[11]

From the moment colonization began, the theology of liberation interprets the history of Latin America as one of dependency.

The sixteenth and seventeenth centuries were marked by a continuation of the evangelization process of the Indians by the church and by the development of an extensive organizational system.[12] The church through its missionaries, clergy, universities, schools, and literature became the primary vehicle for promulgating Iberian culture and values. The period of conquest was followed by a time of relative stability in which the imposed distinctions between native people and the Iberian conquerors became the new norm.[13] The Bourbon period of the eighteenth century saw no innovations but rather an entrenchment of the church as part of the colonial establishment. The expulsion of the Jesuits in the mid-eighteenth

---

8. Theo Tschuy in the review of Hans-Jürgen Prien's *Die Geschichte des Christentums in Lateinamerika*, "Liberation of Latin American Christianity: A Review Article," *Ecumenical Review* 30 (1978) 260.

9. Hans-Jürgen Prien, *Die Geschichte des Christentums in Lateinamerika*, 82.

10. Hart, "Topia and Utopia in Colombia and Peru," 28, and Dussel, *History of the Church in Latin America*, 38, 41.

11. Gustavo Gutiérrez, "Freedom and Salvation: A Political Problem," in *Liberation and Change*, ed. Ronald H. Stone, trans. Alvin Gutterriez (Atlanta: John Knox, 1977) 61.

12. Dussel, "A History of the Church in Latin America," 55–58, describes the organizational structure and, 58–60, the evangelization process.

13. Dussel, *History and the Theology of Liberation*, 89–95.

century (due to their progressive attitudes) discloses the extent of this entrenchment.[14]

COLONIAL WITNESS TO JUSTICE: BARTOLOMÉ DE LAS CASAS

In contrast to the dominant forces of colonial Christendom, the figure of Bartolomé de Las Casas stands in sharp relief.[15] "Bartolomé de Las Casas (1474–1566) was the most well-known name of those who, from the point of view of the gospel and of the poor denounced the conquest and the colonization of the Indians."[16] In 1512 Las Casas was the first Catholic priest ordained in the New World.[17] Although sharing many of the intrinsic presuppositions of colonial Christendom regarding the conversion of the indigenous peoples in order to win their eternal salvation, Las Casas protested against the use of force as a means of provoking conversion and demanded that justice be included in the policy of the church toward the Indians.[18]

Because of this stance, Las Casas received the title "Universal Protector of the Indians of the Indies," a title which he deserved in many ways. For example, Las Casas denounced the "*encomienda* system by which estates were granted in the New World by the Spanish kings which included the subservience of the native peoples living there. He challenged the "*requerimiento*," the method by which conversion was imposed upon the Indians. This method consisted of declaring to the Indians the rights over them which the Pope had granted to Spain and threatening war if they did not accept the faith and submit to Spanish rule. Las Casas also debated against the most well-known sixteenth-century defender of the theology of conquest, advocating just and humane treatment of the Indians commensurate with the gospel message.[19]

---

14. Ibid., 95–96, and Dussel, *History of the Church in Latin America*, 60–61.

15. Gustavo Gutiérrez, *Las Casas: In Search of the Poor of Jesus Christ*, trans. Robert R. Barr (Maryknoll, NY: Orbis, 1993).

16. Gutiérrez, "Freedom and Salvation," 61.

17. Hart, "Topia and Utopia in Colombia and Peru," 30.

18. For this and the following, see Gutiérrez, "Freedom and Salvation," 62–69.

19. Gutiérrez, "Freedom and Salvation," 66–69. See also Hart, "Topia and Utopia in Colombia and Peru," 31–34, and Dussel, *History of the Church in Latin America*, 47–48, 51–52.

Throughout his life, Las Casas witnessed to the rights of the Indian people and advocated non-violent evangelization.[20] References to the work of Bartolomé de Las Casas and other early voices of protest against the injustices of colonial power recur in the writings of the theology of liberation.[21] These advocates of justice, by their persistent defense of the native peoples, are claimed as a redemptive element in the colonial history of the church in Latin America.[22] The witness of Las Casas serves as a symbol of the spirit of liberation theology already in the colonial period.

INDEPENDENCE FROM SPANISH RULE (1808–1825)

The late eighteenth century saw increasing resistance to Spanish exploitation, sometimes in the form of revolutionary movements.[23] The years 1808–1825 define the period in which the Creole (those born in Latin America but of European ancestry) oligarchy revolted and won independence from Spanish rule. During this period, Spain's grip on the colonies was weakened by the need to direct attention to the challenge of Napoleon in Europe. Within Latin America many factors contributed to the growth of the independence movements: resentment by the Creoles of the Spanish economic monopoly, mismanagement of the colonies by the Spanish, the encouragement given to the independence movements by rival powers seeking new economic markets (particularly England), and the growing unrest of the native peoples.[24] It is important to note that these independence struggles did not, however, result in the liberation of the native population. The shifting of power from Spain to the Creole oligarchies within Latin America did not introduce significant change in

---

20. Dussel, *History and the Theology of Liberation*, 84.

21. Other "intrepid champions of justice and proponents of the gospel message of peace" include Antonio de Montesinos, Juan de Yumarraga, Vasco de Quiroga, Juan del Valle, Julian Garces, Jose de Ancheita, as well as "the saints" Toribio de Mogrovejo, Rosa de Lima, Martin de Porres, Pedro Claver, and Luis Beltran, according to "The Final Document" of Puebla, in *Puebla and Beyond: Documentation and Commentary*, ed. John Eagleson and Philip Scharper, trans. John Drury (Maryknoll, NY: Orbis, 1979) 124 (8).

22. Dussel, *History of the Church in Latin America*, 45 and 51–55, emphasizes the positive role taken by many missionaries and bishops throughout the colonial period.

23. Prien, *Geschichte des Christentums in Lateinamerika*, 368–71.

24. J. Andrew Kirk, *Liberation Theology: An Evangelical View from the Third World* (Atlanta: John Knox, 1979) 4. Dussel, *History of the Church in Latin America*, 76–77, especially emphasizes the influence of the expansion of the British Empire.

the overall cultural or religious order.²⁵ At the beginning of this period, the church was sought as an ally for supplying order and unity within the new nations and their rulers. However, the church (apart from some significant exceptions among the clergy) persisted in giving primary loyalty to the original colonial powers. This led the new leaders to a growing alienation from and even hostility against the church.²⁶

THE NEW COLONIALISM (1825–1929)

The securing of independence was followed by a period of organizing the new states around geographical centers and the securing of power by the existing oligarchies.²⁷ National identities were forged which increasingly sought to separate themselves independent from the influence of the church. For example, the constitution of Colombia (1849) proposed the separation of church and state, a remarkable development considering the traditional Latin American pattern of alliance between them. Many of the new governments which arose in the last half of the nineteenth century sought to distance themselves from the former Spanish rule and from the vestiges of Christendom. France became the inspiration for new cultural ideals just as the United States became the inspiration for new technological innovation. Positivism became an influential philosophical viewpoint with an emphasis on reason and law.

Simultaneous with these political and cultural developments was the more gradual shift of economic dependency from Spain to the capitalistic economies of Britain and, increasingly, the United States.²⁸ The liberal governments of Latin America in the nineteenth century by promoting freedom and modernity also opened their countries to the expansion of the free enterprise system. As foreign business interests gained increased influence over the political leadership, a new form of colonialism emerged, one no longer characterized by dependence on Spain but by dependence upon other foreign economic powers. While the ruling

25. Dussel, *History and the Theology of Liberation*, 98–101.

26. Kirk, *Liberation Theology*, 4–11, and Dussel, *History of the Church in Latin America*, 87–94.

27. For this discussion of Latin America in the nineteenth century, see Dussel, *History and the Theology of Liberation*, 101–6, and Dussel, *History of the Church in Latin America*, 48–79, 94–106.

28. Regarding the rise of international capitalism, see Gutiérrez, "Freedom and Salvation," 69–71, and Dussel, *History of the Church in Latin America*, 76–77.

oligarchies profited greatly from this new arrangement, the poor suffered under a new form of oppression.

The church throughout this period sought to maintain the privileges which it possessed under the alliance of throne and altar under Spanish rule.[29] Where the church possessed economic interests, its sought to protect its interests by aligning with the new order. However, the basic intransience of the church in the new political situation led to a growing isolation and withdrawal from political affairs. As the century progressed, the church was attacked by its intellectual opponents for its extreme conservativism. This prompted a defense of traditional dogmatic formulas. The crisis of the church in this period was compounded by an extreme shortage of clergy and members of religious orders, since a new generation was no longer forthcoming from Europe as during Spanish rule. The hesitancy of Rome to recognize the new civil authorities and its favoring a return to the monarchical rule of Spain magnified this problem and prompted increasing animosity toward the church by the state.

THE NEW CHRISTENDOM (1830–1962)

Around 1930, in the midst of the international economic depression and a weakening of the power of the anti-Catholic liberal classes, a new attitude began to manifest itself in the church.[30] An innovative model for defining the church's relationship to the world was proposed, called the "New Christendom."[31] Its purpose was to develop a more positive relationship between the church and the world. The New Christendom movement derived from an intellectual renewal which received its impetus from Jacques Maritain and his book *True Humanism* (1936). The medieval worldview served as the backdrop for this movement [32] with its basic notion of the power of grace at work to perfect nature.[33]

29. For a discussion of the church's attitude in this period, see Kirk, *Liberation Theology*, 8–14, and Dussel, *History of the Church in Latin America*, 78–82, 94–101.

30. Gutiérrez, "Freedom and Salvation," 72–73.

31. Dussel, "Die lateinamerikanische Kirche von Medellin bis Puebla (1968–1979)," in *Lateinamerika*, ed. Prien, 1:72–73, and Dussel, *History of the Church in Latin America*, 106–10.

32. For an extensive discussion of the "New Christendom" model, see Alfredo Fierro, *The Militant Gospel*, trans. John Drury (Maryknoll, NY: Orbis, 1977) 48–75.

33. Gutiérrez, *A Theology of Liberation: History, Politics and Salvation*, trans. Caridad Inda and John Eagleson (Maryknoll, NY: Orbis, 1973) 55.

One significant feature of this model which differentiates it from that of the medieval world was the proposal that the church should operate on two distinct levels, first through evangelization proper and second by Christian inspiration of the temporal sphere.[34] Three basic principles undergirded the New Christendom: "(1) the lay character of political institutions; (2) the underlying Christian inspiration of the state; (3) the full incorporation of non-Christians into the state by virtue of its temporal aims as a civil society."[35] The Church should seek to build a public consensus and permeate the temporal order with Christian values. This was to be achieved particularly through the involvement of Christian laity in society. "The three most significant efforts at mobilizing the church to face the challenge" were "Catholic Action, the Catholic Trade Union Movement, and the Christian Democrat Parties."[36] Through these organizations a burst of enthusiasm and optimism would flow through the church into a society benumbed by years of conservatism and stagnation. In spite of its ambitions, the New Christendom model has been criticized by liberation theologians for its triumphalistic mentality.[37] Although it contributed to a more progressive political outlook, it has been critically evaluated for its timidity, ambiguity, and a failure to propose new social forms.[38]

THE CONCEPT OF DEVELOPMENT

The decade of the 1950s inaugurated the concept of development as a new model for interpreting the economic and social problems of Latin America. Building on the earlier economic theories of Schumpeter and Clark, the findings of the Bandung Conference of 1955 (attended by representatives of many countries especially those from Asia and Africa) recognized the fundamental problem of the impoverished lands to be one of underdevelopment.[39] It was at this conference that the term "Third World" was promulgated to describe those underdeveloped countries which belong neither to the developed capitalist economy of the West nor to the nations

---

34. Ibid., 57.

35. Fierro, *Militant Gospel*, 55.

36. Kirk, *Liberation Theology*, 15. Cf. Dussel, *History of the Church in Latin America*, 216–17, on Christian Democracy in Latin America.

37. Dussel, *History and the Theology of Liberation*, 106.

38. Gutiérrez, *Theology of Liberation*, 56.

39. Ibid., 23.

influenced by the political and economic system of communism.[40] The Bandung Conference was to have initiated the introduction of policies which would lead the Third World out of underdevelopment through the material assistance and moral commitment of the developed world. Underlying the concept of development was the idea of a continuum along which development and underdevelopment were the extreme poles. The object of developmental programs was to speed the process by which the underdeveloped nations could reduplicate the modernization pattern of the developed nations.[41]

Both secular and ecclesiastical structures soon joined forces to cooperate in the development of the Third World. The United Nations declared the first "decade for development" in 1960. A number of international organizations were created: The International Development Bank, International Aid for Development, and the International Money Fund. Prompted by the Bandung Conference, the United Nations also created organizations, such as the United Nations Commission for Trade and Development and the Economic Committee for Latin America, in order to negotiate better terms of trade.[42] Furthermore, "the Alliance for Progress, the Kennedy administration, and the rise of reformist democratic movements in several countries of the continent—notably in Chile, Brazil, Venezuela, Peru, and Colombia—all signaled a new era of hope for peaceful but steady economic and social reform in Latin America."[43] The churches also joined the cause of development: Protestants through the World Council of Churches and various national church bodies; Roman Catholics through the influence of national hierarchies, volunteer programs, and papal encyclicals.[44]

By the middle of the 1960s the model of development became increasingly discredited in Latin America, when the gap between rich and poor nations continued to increase.

---

40. Monika Hellwig, "Liberation Theology: An Emerging School," *Scottish Journal of Theology* 30 (1977) 137.

41. Gutiérrez, *Theology of Liberation*, 83.

42. José Míguez Bonino, *Revolutionary Theology Comes of Age* (London: SPCK, 1975) 24–25.

43. T. Howland Sanks and Brian H. Smith, "Liberation Ecclesiology: Praxis, Theory, Praxis," *Theological Studies* 38 (1977) 5.

44. Hellwig, "Liberation Theology: An Emerging School," 137–38.

> The chasm between the developed and the underdeveloped world was growing wider instead of narrowing, not only because the expected minimum measure of growth was never reached, but because, applied to widely different starting points, even the same rate of growth results in ever-increasing inequality. Foreign investment was taken out of Latin America far more than it has invested. The process of production, distribution, and finance has been almost totally transferred to outside agents (international monopolies). The terms of trade continue to be unfavorable. The prices paid for the use of technology—protected by licenses in the Northern world—far outweighs the benefits of its use. Production has been unable to cope with the increase of population and thus the number and condition of marginals have become worse.[45]

The theory of development has been criticized by the theology of liberation for these inadequacies and has been supplanted by the theory of dependency.[46]

THE CUBAN REVOLUTION (1959)

According to the theologians of liberation the socialist revolution in Cuba pointed toward a new possibility for the future of Latin America beyond developmentalism and reformism.[47] Although representing only a small fraction of the Latin American people, the revolution in Cuba (under the leadership of Fidel Castro) awakened hopes for new political and economic structures.[48] Cuba served for many as symbol for the possible future of Latin America. Especially influential aspects of the Cuban revolution throughout Latin America were the use of guerrilla tactics, reference to Marxism as an interpretive framework, and the establishment of a pattern for socialist society.[49] Cuba's advances in the area of agrarian reform were particularly important.[50]

---

45. Míguez Bonino, *Revolutionary Theology Comes of Age*, 25.

46. Gutiérrez, *Theology of Liberation*, 84–88.

47. Gutiérrez, "Faith as Freedom: Solidarity with the Alienated and Confidence in the Future," *Horizons* 2 (1975) 29, and Dussel, *History of the Church in Latin America*, 161–64.

48. Enrique Dussel, "An International Division of Theological Labor," *Foundations* 23 (1980) 345.

49. Comblin, in *Lateinamerika*, ed. Prien, 2:13.

50. Leopoldo Zea, *Latin American and the World*, trans. Frances K. Hendricks and Beatrice Berler (Norman: University of Oklahoma Press, 1969) 59.

Although Christians took little part in the Cuban revolution,[51] the Roman Catholic Church initially showed a basic openness to the new regime.[52] Shortly thereafter, however, serious tensions developed between state and church when the state required a declaration of adherence to Marxism and nationalized the schools. As a result, "dissatisfaction spread and translated itself in many cases into a radical and complete change of attitude to the revolution."[53] This new attitude resulted in persecution of the church and a drastic reduction in the number of priests and nuns in Cuba. For about ten years the church in Cuba was reduced to silence.[54] Liberation theology remained noticeably uncritical of the persecution against the church which took place at this time.

With the appointment of Cesare Zacchi as Apostolic Nuncio to Cuba, a new attitude emerged, by which church and state increasingly sought to overcome their animosity.[55] Castro at times showed surprising openness to the church as "a strategic ally of socialism in Latin America."[56] The statement of April 1969, in which the Cuban episcopate denounced the economic blockade of Cuba, was indicative of this new attitude.[57]

The struggle of the church in Cuba has been instructive to the theology of liberation regarding the dangers facing the church in relationship to revolution, Marxism, and socialist governments. At the same time, the Cuban revolution also prompted many to view Cuba as an appropriate model for all of Latin America. The decisions of Camilo Torres and Nestor Paz to engage as Christians in guerrilla activity followed the lines drawn by the Cuban revolution.[58] It should be noted that the theology of liberation has emphasized the more favorable aspects of the Cuban revolution with minimal criticism of its abuses.

---

51. Dussel, "International Division of Theological Labor," 348.

52. Rafael Cepeda, "Christian Response to a Revolutionary Situation," *Reformed and Presbyterian World* 28 (1965) 301.

53. Cepeda, "Christian Response to a Revolutionary Situation," 302.

54. Dussel, *History and the Theology of Liberation*, 120–21.

55. Ibid., 121.

56. Dussel, "International Division of Theological Labor," 349. For a more positive appraisal of the relationship of the church to the Castro government, see Kenneth M. Weare, "The Church in Castro's Cuba," *Thought* 59 (1984) 219–28.

57. Dussel, *History and the Theology of Liberation*, 121.

58. Comblin, in *Lateinamerika*, ed. Prien, 2:13.

The Vitality of Liberation Theology

VATICAN II (1962–1965) AND PAPAL ENCYCLICALS (1961, 1963, 1967)

The papacy of John XXIII and the invoking of the Second Vatican Council are of fundamental significance for the attitude which prevailed in the Roman Catholic Church prior to the birth of liberation theology in Latin America. Although the actual Latin American representation at Vatican II was criticized as inadequate, the implications of the Council for the renewal of the Church in the years which followed were monumental.[59] Because the Council took place over a number of years, from 1962 to 1965, the participants themselves underwent a process of transformation during this period.[60] Therefore it is possible to speak of "preconciliar," "conciliar," and "postconciliar" outlooks.[61] It was especially the postconciliar outlook which influenced the emergence of liberation theology. Pope John Paul II remarked that "without Vatican II, the Medellin Conference would have been impossible."[62]

Of the many documents originating at Vatican II,[63] *The Pastoral Constitution on the Church in the Modern World* (*Gaudium et Spes*), with its emphasis on the importance of analyzing social reality, has been particularly important.[64] The church was called upon to envision "as her primary mission the serving of humanity, especially the economically and socially marginated peoples of the world, service designed to make human life more human."[65] In summary, the Second Vatican Council

> urged all Catholics to scrutinize "the signs of the times" and share in the agonies of modern man so as to make the gospel credible to the people of our day, especially to the suffering and oppressed.

---

59. Dussel, *History and the Theology of Liberation*, 111–13, and Dussel, *History of the Church in Latin America*, 139–41.

60. Noggler, in *Lateinamerika*, ed. Prien, 1:21.

61. Fierro, *Militant Gospel*, 12.

62. John Paul II, "Homily at the Basilica of Guadalupe," in *Puebla and Beyond*, ed. Eagleson and Scharper, 74.

63. See Walter M. Abbott, ed., *The Documents of Vatican II* (New York: America, 1966).

64. Noggler, in *Lateinamerika*, ed. Prien, 1:21. For a text of *Gaudium et Spes*, see Joseph Gremillion, *The Gospel of Peace and Justice: Catholic Teaching since Pope John* (Maryknoll, NY: Orbis, 1976) 243–335.

65. Alan Neely, "Liberation Theology in Latin America: Antecedents and Autochthony," *Missiology* 6 (1978) 352.

They had described the Church as the sacrament of mankind's unity, consciously pointing to the Spirit's actions, which go far beyond the institutional framework of the Church itself. Hence the ecclesiological principles of Vatican II were clearly oriented to the service of the world and its struggles for justice and dignity.[66]

Complementing the forces of renewal released in the Roman Catholic world by Vatican II, the encyclical letters of John XXIII and Paul VI added to this new spirit.[67] John XXIII issued two encyclicals of particular importance for Latin America: *Mater et Magistra* (1961), which was important for the way it related the church's social teachings to practical issues (especially economic issues),[68] and *Pacem in Terris* (1963), which gave direction not only to individual life but also to the forms of society and state.[69] Paul VI issued *Populorum Progressio* (1967), which contained criticism of capitalism and called for a form of development which would go beyond the technical and economic model of the developed nations,[70] and also *Humanae Vitae* (1967).[71] It was *Populorum Progressio* which found special resonance within Latin America.[72] While it was also possible from these documents to draw conclusions which were more conservative than those drawn by liberation theology, it was the "liberating" vision of Vatican II and the encyclical letters which served to stimulate the vision of the theologians of liberation.[73]

THE THEOLOGY OF REVOLUTION

During the 1960s considerable attention was given to a "theology of revolution," particularly in Europe and Latin America. The term "theology of revolution" was coined during the Second All-Christian Peace Conference held in Prague in 1964.[74] In the succeeding years a considerable

66. Sanks and Smith, "Liberation Ecclesiology," 5–6.

67. Texts of the following encyclicals are found in Gremillion, *Gospel of Peace and Justice: Mater et Magistra*, 143–200; *Pacem in Terris*, 201–41; *Populorum Progressio*, 387–415; and *Humanae Vitae*, 427–44.

68. Neely, "Liberation Theology in Latin America," 353.

69. Noggler, in *Lateinamerika*, ed. Prien, 1:20.

70. Neely, "Liberation Theology in Latin America," 353.

71. Dussel, in *Lateinamerika*, ed. Prien, 1:77–78.

72. Noggler, in *Lateinamerika*, ed. Prien, 1:22.

73. Neely, "Liberation Theology in Latin America," 353.

74. Robert Banks, "How Revolutionary Is Revolutionary Theology?" *Theology Today* 27 (1971) 394.

literature emerged.⁷⁵ The theology of revolution introduced new and radical themes into theological discourse. Christian advocacy of guerrilla activity, the use of violence as a means of social change, and the advocacy of revolution provoked heated debate. The address of Richard Shaull, as spokesman for the Third World at the World Council of Churches–sponsored World Conference on Church and Society (July 1966 in Geneva), added fuel to this debate.⁷⁶ Although the theology of revolution originated with Latin American writers "for whom revolutionary terminology held no taboo," the theology of revolution became "far more typical of Europe than of Latin America."⁷⁷ As the discussion became increasingly theoretical, interest for a theology of revolution waned in Latin America.⁷⁸ Nevertheless, the theology of revolution marked a turn in theological discussion from an emphasis upon "humanism and existence toward things political."⁷⁹ The theology of revolution served as an important antecedent for the rise of liberation theology.

In this context, it is important to mention the dialogues which took place in Europe between Marxists and Christians in the years 1964–1966.⁸⁰ The literature prompted by these Marxist-Christian encounters adds one additional current to the different streams which fostered the emergence of Latin American liberation theology.

This chapter has analyzed the interpretation of Latin American history from the perspective of liberation theologians. In the next chapter we will examine how liberation theology has engaged and influenced church and society in recent decades in Latin America.

---

75. For comprehensive bibliographies, see Ernst Fiel and Rudolf Weth, eds., *Diskussion zur "Theologie der Revolution"* (Munich: Chr. Kaiser, 1969), and Hans Schöpfer, *Theologie der Gesellschaft: Interdisziplinäre Grundlagen Bibliographie zur Einführung in die befreiungs- und polittheologische Problematik: 1960-1975* (Bern: Peter Lang, 1977).

76. Richard Shaull, "The Revolutionary Challenge to Church and Theology," *Theology Today* 23 (1967) 470-80.

77. Hugo Assmann, *Theology for a Nomad Church*, trans. Paul Burns (Maryknoll, NY: Orbis, 1976) 87.

78. For interpretation and critique of European interest in the theology of revolution, see Assmann, *Theology for a Nomad Church*, 87-92.

79. Fierro, *Militant Gospel*, 12.

80. For brief accounts of the Marxist-Christian dialogues, see Fierro, *Militant Gospel*, 16, and Arthur F. McGovern, *Marxism: An American Christian Perspective* (Maryknoll, NY: Orbis, 1980) 113-14.

3

Emergence and Development of Liberation Theology

BEGINNING IN THE 1960s liberation theology emerged as a considerable force influencing events unfolding in Latin American countries. This chapter will examine the emergence of Latin American liberation theology and trace significant ways it has contributed to both church and society on that continent and across the world.

THE EMERGENCE OF LATIN AMERICAN LIBERATION THEOLOGY (1968)

There were many forces at work in the mid-1960s which influenced the emergence of liberation theology: the New Christendom movement, the rejection of the theory of development, the Cuban revolution, the progressive spirit of Vatican II and the encyclicals which promulgated this spirit, and the debate over a "theology of revolution." The emergence of liberation theology cannot be isolated as a single event but was precipitated by this ferment of forces. It is important, however, to distinguish two major lines of development through which the "theology of liberation" came into existence.

A *first* Protestant line has a number of significant antecedents, especially deriving from the activity and conferences of the World Council of Churches in the years 1948–1968, whose concern for the social implications of Christianity had immediate implications for the Latin American context. One organization related to the World Council of Churches must be singled out for its role in the Protestant stream leading to the emergence of liberation theology: *Iglesia y Sociedad en la America Latina* (ISAL or "Church and Society in Latin America"). This group can also be traced back to the Christian Youth Movement which was created in 1961 at the second Latin American Evangelical Conference.[1] Among the theological concerns addressed by the leaders of the ISAL movement (including Rubem Alves, Emilio Castro, Jose Miguez Bonino, Julio de Santa Ana, and Richard Shaull), three are especially noteworthy for the emergence of liberation theology: the affirmation of the theory of economic dependency, the use of biblical paradigms (for example, the Exodus) for interpreting the Latin American context, and the introduction of the term "liberation" to describe what was needed in light of Latin America's problems.[2]

In giving international attention to the views of ISAL, the role of Richard Shaull was especially significant. His lecture at the World Council of Churches meeting at Geneva in 1966 proposed revolution, guerrilla struggle, and violence as relevant themes for Christian discourse. Also significant was the theological work of Rubem Alves, who completed his doctoral work under Shaull at Princeton in 1968 with the title, *Towards a Theology of Liberation*.

It was through the periodicals, books, and congresses of the ISAL and the presence of its members at various national and international meetings that the questions of violence, guerrilla struggle, and Marxism came to be inseparably connected with liberation theology from its inception.[3] It is interesting to note that these are the exact themes which have been most severely attacked by European and North American critics of liberation theology as they first encountered this particular line of liberation theology. These issues had inordinate influence upon the international discussion of liberation theology. However, it is important to stress that this was only one of the two major lines of development for liberation theology. Moreover, it is the second line of development which had the most influence within Latin America itself.

A *second* line leading to the emergence of liberation theology, Roman Catholic in origin, can be traced to the organization of a large number of

---

1. Alan Neely, "Protestant Antecedents of the Latin American Liberation Theology," PhD diss. (Washington, DC: The American University, 1977) 110–41, 165–208. See also Emilio A. Nunez, "The Theology of Liberation in Latin America," *Bibliotheca Sacra* 134 (1977) 344, and José Comblin, "Theologie der Befreiung in Lateinamerika," in *Lateinamerika: Gesellschaft, Kirche, Theologie*, ed. Hans-Jürgen Prien (Göttingen: Vandenhoeck & Ruprecht, 1981) 2:20.

2. Neely, "Protestant Antecedents of the Latin American Liberation Theology," 197–207, 268–69.

3. Comblin, in *Lateinamerika*, ed. Prien, 2:21.

seminars and movements among Latin American priests (including various worker-priest movements) in the mid-1960s. Notable among these movements were the "Priests for the Third World" in Argentina in 1965[4] and the "National Office of Social Information" (ONIS) in Peru, organized in 1968.[5] In the spirit emanating from Vatican II, attempts were made by priests in these and many other groups to make a connection between the Christian faith and the historical, social, and political situation in Latin America.[6] The authors of the ONIS documents chose the theme of "liberation" as an organizing concept in describing its proposal for Latin American reality.[7]

The work of ONIS is linked by the person of Gustavo Gutiérrez to a small group of theologians who in 1965 began to meet periodically in different Latin American cities.[8] Gathering out of a desire for personal friendship and a common concern for Latin American theology, the group included Juan Luis Segundo, Segundo Galilea, and Lucio Gera along with Gutiérrez. From 1965 to 1970, these authors formulated their central theological viewpoint and began to publish works from the perspective that came to be known as liberation theology. It was in such groups that one can say that liberation theology emerged among Latin American Catholics. The influence of Gustavo Gutiérrez upon the ONIS movement and this small group of theologians (and thereby upon the origins of liberation thought) should be stressed.[9] It was also through the personal involvements of Gutiérrez and Lucio Gera that the perspective

---

4. José Míguez Bonino, *Revolutionary Theology Comes of Age* (London: SPCK, 1975) 50, and Enrique Dussel, *A History of the Church in Latin America: Colonialism to Liberation*, trans. Alan Neely (Grand Rapids: Eerdmans, 1981) 194-98.

5. John William Hart, "Topia and Utopia in Colombia and Peru—The Theory and Practice of Camilo Torres and Gustavo Gutierrez in Their Historical Contexts" (PhD diss., Union Theological Seminary, 1978) 187-90.

6. Cf. Comblin, in *Lateinamerika*, ed. Prien, 2:18, and Dussel, *A History of the Church in Latin America*, 244-45, 326-27. For documents illustrating the ferment within the Latin American church during this period, see *Between Honesty and Hope*, issued by the Peruvian Bishops' Commission for Social Action, trans. John Drury (Maryknoll, NY: Maryknoll Documentation Series, 1970).

7. Gustavo Guttiérez, *A Theology of Liberation*, trans. Caridad Inda and John Eagleson (Maryknoll, NY: Orbis, 1973) 126 n. 43.

8. For the following, see Comblin, in *Lateinamerika*, ed. Prien, 2:20-21.

9. For elaboration of the contribution of Gutiérrez, see Robert McAffee Brown, *Gustavo Gutiérrez* (Atlanta: John Knox, 1980) 24-26.

of liberation theology found prominence in the documents which were produced at Medellín.¹⁰

There is a basic distinction to be made between these two lines of development leading to the theology of liberation.¹¹ In the *first* line (deriving from the ISAL) a highly critical attitude toward the various institutional churches came to prevail.

> The churches could not follow the theological and ideological definition of ISAL and the latter criticized the isolation in which the Protestant churches lived as "cultural enclaves" more closely related to the overseas metropolis than to their own environment.¹²

Correspondingly, Protestant members of ISAL often found themselves condemned, excluded, or regarded with suspicion by their own denominations (while the Roman Catholic members of ISAL were generally no longer recognized by their own church).¹³ Thus alienation and distance from the various institutional churches prevailed in the ISAL.

In the *second* line of development, the theology of liberation developed not in alienation but in connection with the structures of the Roman Catholic Church. These liberation theologians were and remained in good standing with their church and bishops. It is this line which had a particular influence upon the monumental deliberation of the Second Conference of Latin American Bishops held at Medellín in 1968. Although both lines of development share many common concerns (for example, an affirmation of the theory of dependency¹⁴), the contrast in the two outlooks needs to be stressed for a proper understanding of the emergence of liberation theology in Latin America.¹⁵ It is clear in terms of sheer numbers and in terms of impact that the Roman Catholic line of liberation thought has had primary influence throughout Latin America.

Because of the complexity of events which led to the emergence of liberation theology, it is difficult to precisely date its origin. Both Protestant and Roman Catholic antecedents can be traced throughout the decade of the sixties or even earlier. A key year, however, is 1968, based

---

10. Comblin, in *Lateinamerika*, ed. Prien, 2:20–21.
11. Ibid., 2:22.
12. Míguez Bonino, *Revolutionary Theology Comes of Age*, 55.
13. Comblin, in *Lateinamerika*, ed. Prien, 2:22.
14. Ibid., 2:21.
15. Ibid., 2:22.

on number of publications which began to appear at this time and on the preparation process for the Medellín conference held that year.[16] Subsequent to 1968 and the Medellín conference, one should note the growing cooperation between Protestant and Roman Catholic proponents of liberation theology and the merging of their concerns.

CELAM II— MEDELLÍN, COLOMBIA (1968)

The first meeting of the General Conference of CELAM (Latin American Bishops' Conference) in Rio de Janeiro in 1955 had its primary significance in creating a structure which linked the various national episcopacies of Latin America.[17] In the succeeding years the infrastructure of CELAM provided a forum for increased cooperation and the sharing of concerns common to the Roman Catholic Church in Latin America. It was, however, at the Second General Conference held at Medellín, Colombia, from August 24 to September 6, 1968, that the work of the Bishops' Conference attained worldwide significance.

The year 1968 was on many accounts one of turbulent forces. Across the globe there were signs of restlessness: the revolts in France, the racial riots in the United States, and the student movements in many countries.[18] In Latin America itself the revolution in Cuba, the decisions of Che Guevara and Camilo Torres for guerrilla struggle, student strikes, and the crisis of the Christian Democrat regime in Chile are some examples of the widespread disillusionment with reform programs under the developmental model and the system of neocolonialism which it was

---

16. The year 1968 is considered the key year by Míguez Bonino, *Revolutionary Theology Comes of Age*, 30, on the basis of the texts which began to appear then; Gutiérrez, as quoted by Hart, "Topia and Utopia in Colombia and Peru," 189, who states that "the theology of liberation was born two or three months before Medellín"; Dussel, *History and the Theology of Liberation*, trans. John Drury (Maryknoll, NY: Orbis, 1976) 301, and *A History of the Church in Latin America*, 327; and Neely, "Protestant Antecedents of the Latin American Theology of Liberation," 3–4, who traces the earlier Protestant antecedents.

17. Penny Lernoux, "The Long Path to Puebla," in *Puebla and Beyond: Documentation and Commentary*, ed. John Eagleson and Philip Scharper, trans. John Drury (Maryknoll, NY: Orbis, 1979) 10–11. For an elaboration of CELAM I and the period following, see Dussel, *History of the Church in Latin America*, 113–15, 141–43.

18. J. B. Libano, "CELAM III: Fears and Hopes," *Cross Currents* 28 (1978) 21. Cf. Dussel, *A History of the Church in Latin America*, 220–21, regarding student movements in Latin America during this period.

seen to represent.[19] In this milieu the Latin American bishops laid extensive groundwork for Medellín through a process of preparation which included written commentaries upon official declarations of the church (for example, Letter of Sixteen Bishops of the Third World, the documents of Vatican II, and the most recent papal encyclicals), preparatory meetings, and widespread discussion of preparatory documents.[20] The visit of Pope Paul VI to the Eucharistic Conference in Bogotá immediately prior to the opening of CELAM II also focused attention upon the Latin American context.[21]

It is not adequate to interpret the results of the Medellín Conference on the basis of any antecedents.[22] Instead, the Medellín Conference went beyond what anyone might have expected.[23] The 150 bishops and the host of others gathered at Medellín—who included "theological, political, sociological, and other experts; ecumenical observers; workers slaving away often at two or three jobs a day; families from ghettos; labor leaders with their nerve ends in a frazzle; impoverished parish priests; small farmers worried how long their patch of land might sustain them; and underground revolutionaries with their life constantly in danger"—experienced a weeklong process of study, discussion, and dialogue as they labored toward the production of a document.[24] The participants of diverse backgrounds made the Medellín Conference an "event" which became for liberation theology a reference point in the hope for a better future in Latin America.

19. For a description of the historical context at the time of CELAM II, see ibid., 21–22; Hector Borrat, "Liberation Theology in Latin America," *Dialog* 13 (1974) 173–74; T. Howland Sanks and Brian H. Smith, "Liberation Ecclesiology: Praxis, Theory, Praxis," *Theological Studies* 38 (1977) 6; and Phillip E. Berryman, "Latin American Liberation Theology," *Theological Studies* 34 (1973) 358.

20. Cf. Berryman, "Latin American Liberation Theology," 358; Dussel, *History and the Theology of Liberation*, 113–15; and Dussel, *History of the Church in Latin America*, 141–43. The main working draft for the Medellín Conference is in *Between Honesty and Hope*, 171–92.

21. Dussel, *History and the Theology of Liberation*, 114.

22. See Gutiérrez's comment regarding the difference between Medellín and Vatican II in Hart, "Topia and Utopia in Colombia and Peru," 73.

23. Manfred K. Bahmann, "Liberation Theology—Latin American Style," *Lutheran Quarterly* 27 (1975) 144.

24. Dussel, in *Lateinamerika*, ed. Prien, 1:79, contrasts the process of the Medellín Conference to that of Puebla in 1979, which from the start worked toward the production of a final document.

Emergence and Development of Liberation Theology

The sixteen documents which were produced at Medellín[25] seek "to situate the church and theology in the human reality, specifically the reality of oppression and liberation, and in effect say that pastoral work and church structures are to be a function of this human reality."[26] To this end the insights of the social sciences, theology, ethics, and pastoral reflection were employed.[27] In these documents a new outlook prevailed that became the basis for a new attitude.[28] According to the official documents, the signs of the times in Latin America called for a strong critique of the developmental model.[29] Institutionalized violence was named and rejected as a negative force exploiting and oppressing the Latin American people under the present order.[30] The desire for peace was seen to be inseparable from the requirement of justice and the promotion of a new order.[31] The Medellín documents had very definite political implications. The church began to look upon itself in a critical way that attempted to make a break from its alliance with unjust structures[32] and to align itself

---

25. For the official English translation of the Medellín documents, see Louis Michael Colonnese, ed., *The Church in the Present-Day Transformation of Latin America in Light of the Council*, vol. 1, *Position Papers*, and vol. 2, *Conclusions* (Washington, DC: US Catholic Conference, 1970). Four of the documents—"Justice," "Peace," "Family and Demography," and "Poverty of the Church"—are also published in Joseph Gremillion, *The Gospel of Peace and Justice: Catholic Teaching since Pope John* (Maryknoll, NY: Orbis, 1976) 445–76. Of the sixteen Medellín texts, those on "Justice," "Peace," and "Poverty of the Church" are particularly important for the theology of liberation.

26. Berryman, "Latin American Liberation Theology," 359.

27. For analyses and summaries of the Medellin documents, see ibid., 359–64; Hans Schöpfer, *Lateinamerikanische Befreiungstheologie* (Stuttgart: W. Kohlhammer, 1979) 16; and David Abalos, "The Medellin Conference," *Cross Currents* 19 (1969) 113–32.

28. Dussel, *History and the Theology of Liberation*, 114–15, speaks of "a new tone and a new idiom."

29. Medellín Documents: "Peace" (Nos. 8–9), in Gremillion, *The Gospel of Peace and Justice*, 456–57. Cf. also Dussel, in *Lateinamerika*, ed. Prien, 1:78–79; Berryman, "Latin American Liberation Theology," 359–61; and Hart, "Topia and Utopia in Colombia and Peru," 76.

30. Medellín Documents: "Peace" (Nos. 15–16), in Gremillion, *The Gospel of Peace and Justice*, 459–60. Cf. also Penny Lernoux, *Cry of the People* (New York: Penguin, 1980) 38; Sanks and Smith, "Liberation Ecclesiology," 6; and Hart, "Topia and Utopia in Colombia and Peru," 74–79.

31. Medellín Documents: "Peace" (No. 14), in Gremillion, *The Gospel of Peace and Justice*, 458–59. Cf. also Bahmann, "Liberation Theology—Latin American Style," 146–47.

32. Medellín Documents: "Peace" (Nos. 22–29) and "Poverty of the Church" (Nos. 9–11), in Gremillion, *The Gospel of Peace and Justice*, 462, 474. Cf. also Bahmann, "LiberationTheology—Latin American Style," 146.

with the common people, the poor.[33] The church was to become a servant of the poor and to count this service as a pastoral priority. Evangelization and conscientization through base communities and lay movements were to become signs of this new priority.[34] In the words of Hugo Assmann, Medellín "put the stamp of approval on 'liberating language,' using it both in a sociological sense ... and in a theological sense."[35]

By no means was everyone present at Medellín in agreement with the final conclusions.[36] In the years which followed, these same documents, drawing upon their more traditional and less innovative statements, would be employed to counter the church reforms and liberation outlook which also claim Medellín as their precedent. Nonetheless it would be "difficult to exaggerate the importance of Medellín,"[37] in its attempt to be faithful to the situation of the majority of the Latin American people.[38] Medellín became both a sign to the world and a program for the Latin American church.[39] The theology of liberation saw Medellín as a "green light" approving of its theological agenda, and in the next years a period of tremendous theological creativity ensued.[40]

THE PROLIFERATION OF LIBERATION THEOLOGY: CONFERENCES AND LITERATURE

In the years immediately following the Medellín Conference, an explosion of conferences, symposia, and literature dealing with the theology

---

33. Medellín Documents: "Poverty of the Church" (Nos. 1–18), in Gremillion, *The Gospel of Peace and Justice*, 471–76. Cf. also Dussel, in *Lateinamenka*, ed. Prien, 1:80; Sanks and Smith, "Liberation Ecclesiology," 7; Hart, "Topia and Utopia in Colombia and Peru," 78; and Lernoux, in *Puebla and Beyond*, ed. Eagleson and Scharper, 11.

34. Medellín Documents: "Justice" (Nos. 17 and 20) and "Poverty of the Church" (Nos. 12–17), in Gremillion, *The Gospel of Peace and Justice*, 452–53, 474–75. Cf. Berryman, "Latin American Liberation Theology," 362–63; Sanks and Smith, "Liberation Ecclesiology," 6–7; Hugo Assmann, *Theology for a Nomad Church*, trans. Paul Burns (Maryknoll, NY: Orbis, 1976) 46; and Lernoux, *Cry of the People*, 38–40.

35. Assmann, *Theology for a Nomad Church*, 45–46.

36. Cf. Borrat, "Liberation Theology in Latin America," 173; Hart, "Topia and Utopia in Colombia and Peru," 79; and Lernoux, in *Puebla and Beyond*, ed. Eagleson and Scharper, 12.

37. Berryman, "Latin American Liberation Theology," 363.

38. Dussel, in *Lateinamerika*, ed. Prien, 1:79.

39. Noggler, in ibid., 1:57–58.

40. Berryman, "Latin American Liberation Theology," 364.

Emergence and Development of Liberation Theology

of liberation burst forth in Latin America and eventually throughout Europe and North America. This was a time of immense enthusiasm for the vision of liberation theology and optimism about the possibility of liberation within Latin America. A brief accounting of a number of these conferences and symposia indicates the extent to which the theology of liberation flowered during this period. In November 1969, a Theology Congress, held at Mexico City under the auspices of the Archdiocese, grappled with the new concerns raised by the theology of liberation.[41] In March 1970 an international symposium on the theology of liberation was held at Bogotá, resulting in the establishment of a coordinating center, two volumes of quickly prepared essays, and a bulletin titled "Theology of Liberation" which began to circulate privately.[42] After a series of regional meetings, in July 1970 this symposium was repeated with an emphasis on underdevelopment as a form of dependence. Also in July 1970, a gathering of biblical scholars took place at Buenos Aires on the theme "Exodus and Liberation," and many of the papers were later published in the journal *Revista Biblica*.

In August 1970 twenty theologians attended an ecumenical seminar at Buenos Aires on liberation theology and this seminar was repeated the following year. Ciudad Juárez (Mexico) hosted a seminar in October 1970 with several internationally known theologians (Harvey Cox among them), and some of the presentations began to circulate throughout Latin America. In December 1970 nine papers were presented at a theological and pastoral seminar held at Oruro (Bolivia). One of the most well-publicized and influential gatherings, the first Latin American Congress of Christians for Socialism, was held in April 1972 at Santiago (Chile) and will be described in the following section. These are but a sample of the ways in which the theology of liberation began to proliferate throughout Latin America.

Internationally, at El Escorial (Spain) in 1972, a number of papers by liberation theologians were presented, describing Christianity and

---

41. Luis G. del Valle, "Toward a Theological Outlook Starting from Concrete Events," in *Frontiers of Theology in Latin America*, ed. Rosino Gibelli, trans. John Drury (Maryknoll, NY: Orbis, 1979) 79–86

42. For a brief description of this symposium and the following ones, see Assmann, *Theology for a Nomad Church*, 52–53. Monika Hellwig, "Liberation Theology: An Emerging School," *Scottish Journal of Theology* 30 (1977) 140, also describes details of the first Bogotá conference.

social change in Latin America.[43] In the United States, "Theology in the Americas: 1975" was held at Detroit in August as an attempt to discover the significance of Latin American liberation theology for the United States.[44] This gathering has been critically interpreted by many.[45] It served to confront North American theologians with the basic concerns of Latin American liberation theology as well as to confront the Latin American theologians of liberation with the differences in the North American context, especially how the concerns of racism and feminism were raised by theologians from the United States.[46] A second Theology in the Americas conference was held at Detroit in August 1980 and attempted to negotiate the criticisms made of the first conference.[47]

The Ecumenical Association of Third World Theologians was another forum for communicating the concerns of liberation theology. The Latin American participants in this association initially had a dominant influence, but not without a growing sensitivity to the differences between other Third World contexts (Asia and Africa) and Latin America.[48]

International Ecumenical Congresses of Theology were held in Dar es Salaam (Tanzania) in 1976, Accra (Ghana) in 1977, Colombo (Sri Lanka) in 1979, São Paulo (Brazil) in 1980,[49] New Delhi (India) in 1981,

---

43. See Alfred T. Hennelly, "Courage with Primitive Weapons," *Cross Currents* 28 (1978) 11, and Dussel, *A History of the Church in Latin America*, 327.

44. The major presentations and analyses are found in Sergio Torres and John Eagleson, eds., *Theology in the Americas* (Maryknoll, NY: Orbis, 1976).

45. Cf. Gregory Brown, "The Christian Left at Detroit," in *Theology in the Americas*, ed. Torres and Eagleson, 399–429; Alice Hageman, "Liberating Theology Through Action," *Christian Century* 92 (1975) 850–53; Beverly Wildung Harrison, "Challenging the Western Paradigm: The 'Theology in the Americas' Conference," *Christianity and Crisis* 35 (1975) 251–54; Robert McAfee Brown, "Reflections on Detroit," *Christianity and Crisis* 35 (1975) 255–56; Shiela Collins, "Liberation Theology Conference in Detroit," *Journal of Ecumenical Studies* 13 (1976) 183–84; Ronald Martin, "A Look at 'Theology in the Americas,'" *Christianity and Crisis* 38 (1978) 198–200; and James Cone, "From Geneva to São Paulo: A Dialogue between Black Theology and Latin American Liberation Theology," in *The Challenge of Basic Christian Communities*, ed. Sergio Torres and John Eagleson, trans. John Drury (Maryknoll, NY: Orbis, 1981) 267–70.

46. See Torres and Eagleson, eds., *Theology in the Americas*, 177–91, 353–56, 361–76.

47. Cornel West, Caridad Guidote, and Margaret Coakley, eds., *Theology in the Americas II: Conference Papers* (Maryknoll, NY: Orbis, 1982).

48. See Torres and Eagleson, eds., *The Challenge of Basic Christian Communities*, 253–81.

49. Ibid., 231.

Emergence and Development of Liberation Theology

Geneva (Switzerland) in 1983, and Oaxtepec (Mexico) in 1986. The São Paulo meeting especially focused upon Latin American concerns under the theme "Ecclesiology of the Popular Christian Communities." In addition to emphasizing the importance of basic Christian communities and the "irruption of the poor into history," this meeting showed increased awareness of the unique problems of women and blacks in Latin America, indicating responsiveness to the concerns raised at the first "Theology in the Americas" conference.[50] At the Oaxtepec meeting, the Latin American participants further addressed the issues of race, indigenous peoples, and gender.[51] Such opportunities for international dialogue have proven to be a broadening experience for Latin American liberation theologians.

One very significant development ran counter to this proliferation of liberation theology. In the years following Medellín, the various departments within CELAM reckoned with the challenge of liberation theology. But noticeable within CELAM in these years was a growing suspicion by some of the implications of liberation theology. Already at a meeting of presidents and secretaries of the Episcopal Education Commission held in Medellín from late August to early November 1970, growing reservations were voiced to the CELAM hierarchy in a lengthy paper delivered by the General Secretary of CELAM.[52] At the fourteenth ordinary conference of CELAM at Sucre (Bolivia) in November 1972 a decidedly conservative swing within the organization took place.[53] Through a process of restructuring and the election of a predominantly conservative slate of officers, most notably Archbishop Alfonso Lopez Trujillo as General Secretary, there was a significant change in the attitude toward liberation theology. Conservative forces mobilized themselves into what has been described as a "campaign against liberation theology" with support not only within Latin America but also overseas, particularly from Germany.[54]

---

50. The proceedings from this conference are in the volume edited by Torres and Eagleson, *The Challenge of Basic Christian Communities*, and are subtitled "Papers from the International Ecumenical Congress of Theology, Feb. 20–Mar. 2, 1980, São Paulo, Brazil." The emphasis on the concerns of women and blacks are repeated throughout the volume, esp. 24–37 and 46–56.

51. David Tombs, *Latin American Liberation Theology* (Boston: Brill, 2002) 224.

52. Assmann, *Theology for a Nomad Church*, 53, 106 n 8.

53. Dussel, in *Challenge of Basic Christian Communities*, ed. Torres and Eagleson, 82–83.

54. Ibid., 82, and Dussel, in *Lateinamerika*, ed. Prien, 1:95.

> The Sucre Conference criticized liberation theology, the Latin American Pastoral Institute (IPLA), and the church's option for the poor. Thus the church was left without a critical voice on the continental level—though not on local or national levels.[55]

In the meetings of the Synod of Bishops in the years 1974 and 1977, the conservative reaction continued to grow.[56] In the preparations for and holding of the Third General Conference of CELAM in Puebla (Mexico) in 1979 the influence of this conservativism became evident.[57] The increasing conservativism within CELAM during these years had its parallel in the growing conservativism among several Latin American governments during this period.[58]

In conclusion, it is not possible to recount the number of meetings, groups, and publications dealing with liberation theology in the years following Medellín. The proliferation of books, articles, journals, and unpublished manuscripts on liberation theology within Latin America, Europe, and North America testify to the rapid growth of the liberation perspective. Virtually all major theological periodicals published articles discussing liberation theology. In some cases whole issues were devoted to this topic.[59] Worthy of special mention for its worldwide influence was the publication of Gustavo Gutiérrez, *A Theology of Liberation*, in Spanish in 1971 and in English translation in 1973.[60] The theological work of Gutiérrez is but the most well-known of the many serious contributions

---

55. Dussel, in *Challenge of Basic Christian Communities*, ed. Torres and Eagleson, 83.

56. Ibid., 81.

57. Cf. Hennelly, "Courage with Primitive Weapons," 11, and Lernoux, in *Puebla and Beyond*, ed. Eagleson and Scharper, 20–25.

58. Dussel, in *The Challenge of Basic Christian Communities*, ed. Torres and Eagleson, 83–93.

59. Full issues of periodicals devoted to liberation theology in the English language include *Christianity and Crisis* 33 (Sept 17, 1973) and 33 (Oct 15, 1973) on "Liberation Theology and Christian Realism"; *Concilium 96: The Mystical and Political Dimension of the Christian Faith*, ed. Claude Geffre and Gustavo Gutiérrez (New York: Herder & Herder, 1974); *Dialog* 13 (Summer 1974) on "Liberation Theology and the Third World"; *International Review of Mission* 66 (January 1977) on "Ministry with the Poor"; *Cross Currents* 28 (Spring 1978) on "Puebla: Moment of Decision for the Latin American Church"; *Theological Education* (Autumn 1979) on "Theological Education and Liberation Theology: A Symposium"; and *Foundations* 23 (Oct–Dec 1980) on "peoples' church."

60. Gustavo Gutiérrez, *Teología de la liberación: Perspectivas* (Lima: CEP, 1971) and in English translation, *A Theology of Liberation: History, Politics and Salvation*, trans. Caridad Inda and John Eagleson (Maryknoll, NY: Orbis, 1973).

Emergence and Development of Liberation Theology

by liberation theologians who elaborated their perspective during this highly creative period. As the decade of the 1970s continued, the theology of liberation increasingly had to deal with the opposing and even reactionary forces.

CHRISTIANS FOR SOCIALISM (APRIL 1972)

Perhaps the most controversial, well-publicized, and instructive of the movements at work in Latin America in the early 1970s was "Christians for Socialism." This movement arose in Chile during the presidency of Salvador Allende between 1970 and 1973.[61] The group first became widely known in April 1971 for the "Declaration of the 80," a statement by eighty priests committing themselves as Christians to the implementation of socialism.[62] In the following months, plans were made to hold a convention for those Latin American Christians "who regarded socialism as a necessary precondition for the construction of a just and humane society."[63] The stated objectives included the desire to analyze the concrete experiences of revolutionary Christians in Latin America, to give public expression to this revolutionary option, and to provide for sharing between various groups involved in the revolutionary struggle.[64] From its inception the Christians for Socialism movement participated in a critical exchange with the hierarchy of the Chilean Episcopate.[65] The political activity of priests, the option for Marxism, and accusations about inadequate theology were prominent concerns expressed by the hierarchy. It was made clear that the upcoming convention was neither sponsored nor approved by the church leadership.[66]

---

61. For historical background regarding Chile during the Allende period, see "Exploring the Meaning of Liberation," in *Theology in the Americas*, ed. Torres and Eagleson, 217–20.

62. "Declaration of the 80," in *Christians and Socialism: Documentation of the Christians for Socialism Movement in Latin America*, ed. John Eagleson, trans. John Drury (Maryknoll, NY: Orbis, 1975) 3–6.

63. "Draft Agenda," in Eagleson, ed., *Christians and Socialism*, 17.

64. Ibid., 21–22.

65. "Movement—Hierarchy Dossier," in Eagleson, ed., *Christians and Socialism*, 33–66.

66. "Authorized Summary of Cardinal Silva's Views," in Eagleson, ed., *Christians and Socialism*, 64–66.

The Vitality of Liberation Theology

On April 23–30, 1972, at Santiago, Chile, the "First Convention of Christians for Socialism" was held. Over four hundred delegates gathered from Chile and throughout Latin America, including some Protestant representatives (from ISAL) and observers from Europe and North America.[67] A majority were priests. Prominent among the theologians were Hugo Assmann and Gustavo Gutiérrez. After initial emphasis on national reports and the sharing of regional issues, attention was focused upon the work of various sub-committees, one of which drafted the Final Document approved by the convention.[68] In this document it was clear that socialism itself was not a question for discussion. Rather, the question was how to carry out the existing commitment to socialism in Latin America. It was perceived that only two options existed for the future of Latin America: either the existing state of exploitative dependency or socialism. Through the use of dependency theory and class analysis, cooperation with Marxists for a socialist future was understood as a necessary choice for Christians who wished to side with the poor and oppressed. The political-ideological nature of this struggle was affirmed. The Christian faith was called upon to act as "a critical and dynamic leaven for revolution."[69] Thus participants in the Christians for Socialism movement opted for political, even revolutionary, struggle as a necessary part of their faith in light of the Latin American reality.

The Christians for Socialism movement was widely criticized for being naive, overly optimistic, impatient, doctrinally weak, idealistic, or opportunistic. One of the most extensive critiques was from the Chilean bishops who defended the church's moral position and authority against the decision for Marxism, class struggle, and partisan politics.[70] This conflict between the hierarchy and the Christians for Socialism movement indicates the tensions which developed within the Roman Catholic Church during the 1970s. Finally, the decision was made by the hierarchy

---

67. Hector Borrat, "Liberation Theology in Latin America," 174, and Joseph R. Barndt, "Revolutionary Christians Confer in Santiago," *Christian Century* 89 (1972) 691–95.

68. "Final Document of the Convention," in Eagleson, ed., *Christians and Socialism*, 160–75.

69. Ibid., 172.

70. "Christian Faith and Political Activity: Declaration of the Chilean Bishops," in Eagleson, ed., *Christians and Socialism*, 179–228.

to deny priests and members of religious orders membership in the organization.⁷¹

The Christians for Socialism movement demonstrates how the urgency of the Latin American situation of poverty and oppression called for a new and radical response by many Christians, a response which led them to new alliances and daring to speak openly about the need for revolution. The movement represents the choice of an extreme option, yet one which many Christians felt compelled to make in light of the Latin American reality. The existence of this movement was cut short by the military coup of September 11, 1973, when the Allende government was toppled and the Christians for Socialism movement outlawed.

GROWING REPRESSION (1970s)

The September 1973 overthrow of the Allende government in Chile was representative of a growing tide of repressive governments sweeping through Latin America in the mid-1970s.⁷² The coups in Brazil in 1964, Argentina in 1966, and Peru in 1968 were followed by a dramatic swing toward rightist governments in the 1970s: the coup in Bolivia and the rule of Banzer (August 21, 1971), the dissolution of the Uruguayan Congress (June 27, 1973), the coup in Chile and the Pinochet rule (September 11, 1973), the rule of Morales Bermudez in Peru (August 28, 1975), the fall of the nationalist military government in Ecuador (January 13, 1976), and the fall of Peron to General Videla in Argentina (March 24, 1976).⁷³ These new governments, when seen in conjunction with the already existing rule of Stroessner in Paraguay, Duvalier in Haiti, and Belaguer in Santo Domingo and the military dictatorships under the pretense of democracy in Guatemala, Honduras, El Salvador, and Nicaragua, paints a picture of repression that stood in sharp contrast to the hopes raised at Medellín and the growth of liberation theology.⁷⁴

---

71. Ibid., 216–17.

72. Berryman, "Doing Theology in a (Counter-) Revolutionary Situation: Latin American Liberation Theology in the Mid-Seventies," in *Theology in the Americas*, ed. Torres and Eagleson, 54.

73. For these dates and events, see Dussel, in *Challenge of Basic Christian Communities*, ed. Torres and Eagleson, 79–80, and Dussel, *History of the Church in Latin America*, 148–60, 224–27.

74. For a brief description of the governments existing in Paraguay, Brazil, Peru, Bolivia, Ecuador, Chile, Argentina, and Uruguay in the 1970s, see Hans Schöpfer, *Theologie*

One of the most influential theories used to support this swing to the right was "national security."[75] National security theory, having originated as a part of US foreign policy, was adopted by several Latin American governments during this period. The roots of national security as a part of US policy dates back to the presidency of Truman and the founding of the National Security Council and the Central Intelligence Agency in 1947. It found growing importance in relationship to the Korean War, expanded during the Kennedy administration in response to the Cuban crisis, developed further during the presidencies of Johnson and Nixon in response to the Vietnam War, and also during the presidency of Carter with the formation of the Trilateral Commission.[76] Based upon worldwide strategy and a geopolitical outlook, a central concern of national security theory was to curb communist influence throughout the world. The world was understood as the arena for a perpetual struggle between opposing world powers with the survival of the free state as the ultimate goal. Liberation theologians criticized the ideological role of this theory in defending US corporate and military interests.

In Latin America, the theory of national security was promoted by military and authoritarian governments as a way of combating communism and defending US interests. According to Rockefeller's "Report on the Americas" in 1969, Brazil was singled out by President Nixon as a test case which would be decisive for the future of Latin America.[77] Billions of dollars in foreign aid and military armaments were invested in Brazil's "one-party state in order to protect 'national security' and 'profit and stability' in the global war between communism and the West."[78] Social, political, and economic rights were regularly sacrificed in the effort to oppose subversive influences and threats of communism whether they

---

der Gesellschaft: Interdisziplinäre Grundlagen Bibliographie zur Einführung in die befreiungs- und polittheologische Problematik: 1960-1975 (Bern: Peter Lang, 1977) 50-52.

75. Comblin, in *Lateinamerika*, ed. Prien, 2:14, and Dussel, *History of the Church in Latin America*, 130-32. For an analysis of the theory and methods of the national security state, see José Comblin, *The Church and the National Security State* (Maryknoll, NY: Orbis, 1979) 64-98.

76. Schöpfer, *Lateinamerikanische Befreiungstheologie*, 66-68, and Dussel, *A History of the Church in Latin America*, 229-30.

77. Lernoux, in *Puebla and Beyond*, ed. Eagleson and Scharper, 15-16. Schöpfer, *Lateinamerikanische Befreiungstheologie*, 70-82, describes Brazil as a model for all of Latin America.

78. Lernoux, in *Puebla and Beyond*, ed. Eagleson and Scharper, 15.

Emergence and Development of Liberation Theology

came from political parties, labor unions, the press, universities, churches, or other groups and individuals.[79] Support for national security states by the United States was continued in other countries throughout Latin America.[80]

National security theory spread by the US training of Latin American army personnel[81] and through the influence of the U.S. Central Intelligence Agency.[82] One action in which the CIA played a major role was the "Banzer plan" in Bolivia in which progressive bishops were to be harassed and foreign priests and nuns arrested and expelled.[83] A similar plan was later adopted by ten other Latin American governments.[84] In sum, the theory of national security has served as an umbrella term for a policy which promoted military and authoritarian governments ruling in an "emergency" situation under the suspension of civil rights in order to combat the influence of communism and promote economic development by the free enterprise system.[85] The wealthy ruling classes and the military governments, in cooperation with multinational corporations and banks, obtained significant economic advantages under the protection of governments devoted to preserving national security.[86]

While repressive forces were taking hold in many Latin American countries, conservative forces were also increasing pressure on the Latin American church. Reservations about the new direction of the church at Medellín were growing, especially among the most conservative hierarchies.[87] On the international level, changes in the Pontifical Commission on Justice and Peace, the end of the progressive periodical *Publik* in Germany, and the removal of Father Louis Colonnese as director of

---

79. Ibid., 16. Lernoux also gives extensive documentation to the struggle for human rights in Latin America in *Cry of the People*.

80. Schöpfer, *Lateinamerikanische Befreiungstheologie*, 82–84, gives examples of the use of national security theory in Colombia, Argentina, Uruguay, Chile, and Bolivia.

81. Schöpfer, *Lateinamerikanische Befreiungstheologie*, 66, and Lernoux, in *Puebla and Beyond*, ed. Eagleson and Scharper, 9.

82. Lernoux, *Cry of the People*, 281–310.

83. Ibid., 142–45; Lernoux, in *Puebla and Beyond*, ed. Eagleson and Scharper, 17; and Schöpfer, *Lateinamerikanische Befreiungstheologie*, 62–64.

84. Lernoux, *Cry of the People*, 145.

85. Cf. Schöpfer, *Lateinamerikanische Befreiungstheologie*, 65–66.

86. Lernoux, in *Puebla and Beyond*, ed. Eagleson and Scharper, 16.

87. Libano, "CELAM III," 23.

the Catholic Inter-American Cooperation Program were indicators of a changing mood.[88] Within Latin America the changes in CELAM under the leadership of General Secretary Lopez Trujillo were considerable. Among those measures which were described as a "campaign of CELAM" against the theology of liberation were the replacement of liberation theologians by its opponents in the Pastoral Institute founded at Medellín, the organization of theological congresses at which liberation theology was opposed, and the increasingly polemical stance against liberation theology evidenced in CELAM supported publications.[89] Catholic movements such as "Tradition, Family, and Property" were supported during this period and found favor by military governments as a Roman Catholic voice more compatible with their interests.[90] Smear campaigns, para-police harassment, and attempts to expel foreign clergy and bishops were used as tactics.[91]

Opposition to the theology of liberation was also the goal of foreign-financed campaigns waged in Latin America under the direction of the Belgian Jesuit Roger Vekemans. Vekemans was transferred from his position teaching sociology at Rome in 1957 to a position training Jesuits in Chile and initially participated in several reform measures. However, due to his anti-communist sentiment, Vekemans developed into an influential opponent of liberation theology.[92] Through the 1960s, Vekemans received financial support for his Centro Bellarmino (Center for Research and Social Action), first from the West German bishops and government and later from the Alliance for Progress and the Central Intelligence Agency.[93] Increasingly, Vekemans was approached by the CIA for information and help in opposing the threat of communism. Leaving Chile upon the election of Allende in 1970, Vekemans organized the Research Center for

88. Dussel, in *Challenge of Basic Christian Communities*, ed. Torres and Eagleson, 81.

89. Comblin, in *Lateinamerika*, ed. Prien, 2:30–32. Cf. also Alfonso Lopez Trujillo, *Liberation or Revolution? An Examination of the Priest's Role in the Socioeconomic Class Struggle in Latin America* (Huntington, IN: Our Sunday Visitor, 1977) 59–65, 74–77, in which the author equates liberation theology with the Christians for Socialism movement and Marxism. Lopez Trujillo insists on the "neutrality" and non-involvement of priests in things political, 105–8.

90. Comblin, in *Lateinamerika*, ed. Prien, 2:32, and Lernoux, *Cry of the People*, 293–304.

91. Lernoux, in *Puebla and Beyond*, ed. Eagleson and Scharper, 17.

92. Lernoux, *Cry of the People*, 25–26.

93. Ibid., 26.

the Development and Integration of Latin America (CEDIAL) in Bogotá.[94] Through CEDIAL and publications such as *Tierra Nueva*, Vekemans organized an attack upon the theology of liberation.[95] Important contacts for Vekemans were Cardinal Sebastiana Baggio, prefect of the Sacred Congregation of Bishops and president of the Pontifical Commission for Latin America in Rome, and CELAM's General Secretary Lopez Trujillo.[96]

The campaign against liberation theology and other progressive movements in the Latin American church was formalized in March 1976 at a meeting in Rome of the "Church and Liberation Circle of Studies," a meeting cosponsored by the Roman Curia and Adveniat, the German bishops' aid agency for the Latin American Church.[97] Several German theologians took part as well as Latin American theologians known to be opponents of liberation theology.[98] Among the arguments employed by Vekemans for opposing liberation theology was his equation of the Christians for Socialism movement in Chile with the essence of the theology of liberation, employing the Final Document of the 1972 Christians for Socialism convention as a summary of liberation theology, together with a critique of the use of Marxism.[99]

A strong reaction against the use of Adveniat to support the work of Vekemans in his opposition to the theology of liberation was published by over one hundred German theologians in November 1977.[100] In addition to protesting the activities of Vekemans and Lopez Trujillo, the German theologians called for an accounting by Adveniat (and in particular by Bishop Franz Hengsbach, Adveniat's director) for its role in the campaign.[101] In spite of such denunciations, Adveniat continued its attack on liberation theology and was supported in its efforts by financial support from a Catholic organization in Milwaukee called the De Rance Foundation.[102]

94. Ibid., 27.
95. Comblin, in *Lateinamerika*, ed. Prien, 2:28.
96. Lernoux, in *Puebla and Beyond*, ed. Eagleson and Scharper, 21.
97. Ibid. See also Comblin, in *Lateinamerika*, ed. Prien, 2:28.
98. Comblin, in *Lateinamerika*, ed. Prien, 2:28.
99. For an elaboration of these tactics as employed by Vekemans, see ibid., 29–30.
100. English translation published as "We Must Protest," *Cross Currents* 28 (1978) 66–70.
101. "We Must Protest," 69–70.
102. Lernoux, in *Puebla and Beyond*, ed. Eagleson and Scharper, 22.

The Vitality of Liberation Theology

The list of those individual groups, priests, and bishops who were harassed, arrested, tortured, expelled, and even put to death under the wave of repression flooding Latin America during the 1970s is vast.[103] Repression both by governments and those within the church led to a change of mood among the theologians of liberation. Assmann spoke of a farewell to the euphoria which characterized the church immediately following Medellín.[104] One commentator described the next task as "doing theology in a (counter-) revolutionary situation."[105] The themes of martyrdom,[106] persecution,[107] "captivity," and "exile"[108] increased in importance under these new conditions. Also, the question of human rights took on new and pointed significance. This historical background shaped the theology of liberation in the period leading to the third General Conference of CELAM in Puebla, Mexico, in 1979.

CELAM III—PUEBLA, MEXICO (1979)

The Third General Conference of CELAM, held at Puebla, Mexico, from January 27 to February 13, 1979, needs to be interpreted in the full context of events and influences which took place prior to and during the conference itself.[109] In the process leading up to Puebla, the General Secretary of CELAM, Lopez Trujillo, sought to reverse the progressive tide

---

103. Names of the "martyred" between 1964 and 1978 are in Lernoux, *Cry of the People*, 463–69.

104. Assmann, *Theology for a Nomad Church*, 99.

105. Berryman, in Torres and Eagleson, eds., *Theology of the Americas*, 54.

106. Jon Sobrino, "The Witness of the Church in Latin America," in *Challenge of Basic Christian Communities*, ed. Torres and Eagleson, 170–80.

107. Lernoux, in *Puebla and Beyond*, ed. Eagleson and Scharper, 17–18.

108 Cf. Leonardo Boff, "Christ's Liberation via Oppression: An Attempt at Theological Construction from the Standpoint of Latin America," in *Frontiers of Theology in Latin America*, ed. Rosino Gibellini, trans. John Drury et al. (Maryknoll, NY: Orbis, 1983) 125–30; Comblin, in *Lateinamerika*, ed. Prien, 2:26; and Dussel, *History of the Church in Latin America*, 327–29.

109. Dussel, in *Challenge of Basic Christian Communities*, ed. Torres and Eagleson, 94, and Dussel, *History of the Church in Latin America*, 229–31, divides the process into four segments: (1) the convocation of the conference, November 30, 1976, to the appearance of the preparatory document, November 1977; (2) from the appearance of the preparatory document to the publication of the working draft document, September 1978; (3) from the publication of the working draft until the start of the conference, January 27, 1979 (includes the delay prompted by the death of John Paul I); and (4) the Puebla conference itself ending February 13, 1979.

released at the Medellín Conference and to cease the influence of liberation theology.[110] The reorganization of CELAM and the influence given to the ideas of Vekemans were indicative of a dramatic change of attitude within CELAM under its new leadership.[111] Thus it was not a surprise when on November 30, 1977, the 214-page preparatory document for Puebla, written by Lopez Trujillo and a staff of conservative sociologists and theologians, expressed their opposition to liberation theology and sought to alter the direction of Medellín.[112] In this document the theory of development was revived to explain the problems of Latin America. It avoided condemning human rights violations, abuses by multinational corporations, and the threat posed by national security states. The church's role was to maintain a traditional Catholic society and to give the poor hope and consolation in a better hereafter.[113]

Negative reaction to the document, not only by liberation theologians but also by bishops, priests, religious, basic Christian communities, peasants, and natives, was spontaneous and overwhelming.[114] A substantial literature critical of the preparatory document developed rapidly.[115] The rejection of the document by a majority of the bishops conferences and even by many conservative bishops led to the rewriting of the document in mid-1978 by a small team of moderate bishops under the direction of Cardinal Aloisio Lorscheider. The result of their revision was a shorter, more concise document which employed language from the Medellín documents especially regarding the church's commitment to

110. Dussel, in *Challenge of Basic Christian Communities*, ed. Torres and Eagleson, 93–95.

111. Lernoux, *Cry of the People*, 413–14.

112. Comblin, in *Lateinamerika*, ed. Prien, 2:34; Lernoux, in *Puebla and Beyond*, ed. Eagleson and Scharper, 23; and Dussel, *A History of the Church in Latin America*, 230–31.

113. Dussel, in *Challenge of Basic Christian Communities*, ed. Torres and Eagleson, 94, and Lernoux, in *Puebla and Beyond*, ed. Eagleson and Scharper, 23.

114. Dussel, in *Challenge of Basic Christian Communities*, ed. Torres and Eagleson, 94.

115. For example, Dussel, ibid., 94–95, mentions two alternative documents presented in opposition. See also Gustavo Gutiérrez, "The Preparatory Document for Puebla: A Retreat from Commitment," *Christianity and Crisis* (Sept 18, 1978) 211–18, and the entire issue of *Cross Currents* 28.1 (Spring 1978), particularly the contributions by Richard, 43–46; a group of Peruvian theologians, 47–54; Helder Camara, 55–59; and the Costa Rican Ecumenical Council, 60–65.

the poor and oppressed.[116] The process of debate, discussion, and rewriting proved fruitful in involving a broad segment of the church prior to Puebla. This may not have been possible without the delay of the start of the conference (originally October 1978) necessitated by the death of Pope John Paul I in August 1978. Otherwise the Puebla conference may have started on time and allowed a different result.[117]

The opening of Puebla took place in the wake of the five-day visit of Pope John Paul II to Mexico during which he delivered a total of over forty addresses. An estimated twenty million people were captivated by the charisma of the newly elected pope, the first non-Italian in five centuries to hold this office.[118] The evaluations of the pope's visit and especially of his speeches have been varied.[119] Those emphasizing his initial addresses noted their conservative tone and considered them a retreat from Medellín and even an attack upon liberation theology.[120] At least one interpreter suggested that this conservativism should be attributed not to the pope himself but to his advisors.[121] By contrast, the later addresses of the pope, particularly the "Address to the Indians of Oaxaca and Chiapas," spoke clearly of the suffering and unjust treatment of the poor and referred to "a social mortgage on all private property."[122] It appeared that Pope John Paul II was changed by his encounter with the people and the poverty of Latin America.

Those sympathetic to the theology of liberation have been highly critical about a number of matters surrounding the preparation of the conference itself. The location of the conference at Puebla hearkened

---

116. Lernoux, in *Puebla and Beyond*, ed. Eagleson and Scharper, 23–24.

117. Dussel, in *The Challenge of Basic Christian Communities*, ed. Torres and Eagleson, 94.

118. Moises Sandoval, "Report from the Conference," in *Puebla and Beyond*, ed. Eagleson and Scharper, 32. See also Lernoux, *Cry of the People*, 425–32, and Dussel, *A History of the Church in Latin America*, 231–32, for details of the pope's visit.

119. For the texts of the addresses by John Paul II, see Eagleson and Scharper, eds., *Puebla and Beyond*, 47–83.

120. Sandoval, in Eagleson and Scharper, eds., *Puebla and Beyond*, 32–33.

121. Jon Sobrino, "The Significance of Puebla for the Catholic Church in Latin America," in *Puebla and Beyond*, ed. Eagleson and Scharper, 292.

122. John Paul II, "Address to the Indians of Oaxaca and Chiapas," in *Puebla and Beyond*, ed. Eagleson and Scharper, 82. See also the comments of Dussel, *A History of Theology in Latin America*, 235–36, regarding the people's experience of Pope John Paul II at Oaxaca.

Emergence and Development of Liberation Theology

back to an era when the church remained untouched by "the disrupting tides of a troubled civilization."[123] The location, in a highly conservative city filled with numerous churches and cathedrals, was carefully chosen by the CELAM leadership.[124] Especially ominous was the stone wall (ten feet high) surrounding the seminary where the conference met.[125] Tight security measures were enacted to limit entrance exclusively to delegates, press, and staff. The selection of delegates had been carefully guided by Lopez Trujillo and Cardinal Baggio of the Vatican. In addition to the conservative CELAM staff and the conservative or moderate delegates from the bishoprics who participated in Puebla, an additional 117 delegates—twelve with vote—had been appointed by John Paul I and confirmed by John Paul II according to the recommendations of Baggio and Lopez Trujillo.[126] Especially noteworthy was the decision that the "periti" (or experts) supplied to the bishops as a guide to their discussions were to be appointed by the pope rather than chosen by the bishops themselves as had been the case at Medellín. Thus, most of Latin America's best-known theologians, especially those sharing the perspective of liberation theology, were officially excluded from the total of 350 delegates, observers, experts, and other representatives allowed entrance to the conference.[127]

The conference opened with a homily at the January 27 mass and an opening address the following day by John Paul II. His address emphasized many concerns which would be incorporated into the final document of Puebla.[128] From the very start of the Puebla Conference, the production of the Final Document was given top priority. A revision of the agenda proposed by Lopez Trujillo indicated early in the conference that a progressive element was still represented at Puebla.[129] Various measures designed to exclude the viewpoint of liberation theology and Medellín's option for

---

123. Sandoval, in Eagleson and Scharper, eds., *Puebla and Beyond*, 29.
124. Lernoux, *Cry of the People*, 433–34, describes the Puebla setting.
125. Sandoval, in Eagleson and Scharper, eds., *Puebla and Beyond*, 29.
126. Ibid., 30.
127. Ibid., 31.
128. John Paul II, "Homily at the Basilica of Guadalupe" and "Opening Address at the Puebla Conference," in *Puebla and Beyond*, ed. Eagleson and Scharper, 72–76, 57–71. See also Virgilio Elizondo, "The Pope's Opening Address: Introduction and Commentary," in ibid., 47–55.
129. Lernoux, *Cry of the People*, 433, and Dussel, in *Challenge of the Basic Christian Communities*, ed. Torres and Eagleson, 95.

the poor were frustrated. Although the liberation theologians were denied access to the conference itself, it proved impossible to deny exit to the progressive bishops and delegates.[130] Having consulted with their own experts, they returned to the meeting with insights and position papers by liberation theologians which circulated throughout the convention.[131] Eighty-four position papers for the twenty-one various commissions were circulated by the liberation theologians and social scientists working outside the conference. It has been estimated that perhaps 25 percent or more of the Final Document can be attributed to this source.[132] Evidence for the machinations of Lopez Trujillo was a letter dictated by him to a conservative bishop within CELAM prior to the conference which indicated his plans to manipulate Puebla.[133]

It was the moderates, moved by the testimony of bishops such as Paulo Evaristo Arns and Oscar Romero together with the witness of those having experienced persecution in countries such as Argentina and El Salvador, who prevailed in the Final Document in its approved form.[134] Though the Final Document contains ambiguities and can be interpreted variously, the basic thrust of Medellín was not denied but reaffirmed.[135] Especially strong was the document's analysis of the underlying roots of Latin American poverty, in which the role of economic systems, multinational corporations, the arms race, and the need for structural reform are emphasized.[136] The document also affirms "A Preferential Option for the Poor"[137] and articulates a vision of "Church Activity on Behalf of the Person in National and International Society."[138] The structural dimensions of Latin American poverty, injustice, and violations of human

---

130. Lernoux, *Cry of the People*, 434.

131. Sandoval, in Eagleson and Scharper, eds., *Puebla and Beyond*, 35.

132. Ibid., 36.

133. Lernoux, *Cry of the People*, 435, and Dussel, *History of the Church in Latin America*, 232.

134. Lernoux, *Cry of the People*, 436. See also Dussel, *History of the Church in Latin America*, 231, for a description of the conflicting forces at Puebla.

135. "Evangelization in Latin America's Present and Future. Final Document of the Third General Conference of the Latin American Episcopate," in *Puebla and Beyond*, ed. Eagleson and Scharper, 122–285. References to the Medellín documents are interspersed throughout.

136. "Evangelization in Latin America's Present and Future," 131 (Nos. 63–68).

137. Ibid., 264–67 (Nos. 1134–65).

138. Ibid., 278–82. (Nos. 1254–93).

rights are emphasized. Throughout the main body of the text, in discussing the theme of "evangelization," the liberation point of view appears in the midst of more traditional concerns dealing with the inner life of the church and its relationship to the Latin American context.

The evaluations of the Final Document by those supportive of liberation theology have been overwhelmingly positive.[139] This was remarkable in light of the efforts taken to secure the opposite result. Many reviewers judged that the Puebla document stood firmly in the tradition of Medellín, particularly in its affirmation of the church's option for the poor and the significance of the basic Christian communities for Latin America. A new emphasis was the critical stance toward the national security ideology that arose in Latin America after Medellín.

In conclusion, it is important to note that the importance of Puebla as an "event" transcends the written "text" of the conference.[140] In this regard Puebla continued to be appropriated by the church in the years to follow. Although the control of CELAM remained in the hands of those opposed to the liberation perspective,[141] the events at Puebla indicated that liberation theology would continue to be a vital force within the Latin American church.

THE REVOLUTION IN NICARAGUA (1979)

The overthrow of the Nicaraguan dictator Anastasio Somoza Debyle on July 19, 1979, as leader of one of Latin America's most oppressive regimes became a focal point for the hopes of liberation in Latin America in the early 1980s. The revolutionary movement in Nicaragua was called the "Sandinista Front," named after the thought and example of the freedom fighter Augusto Cesar Sandino. In the late 1920s and early 1930s, Sandino identified with the poor in opposing and fighting against US control

---

139. For example, Lernoux, *Cry of the People*, 437–43; Harvey Cox and Faith Annette Sand, "What Happened at Puebla?" *Christianity and Crisis* 39 (1979) 57–60; Dussel, *History of the Church in Latin America*, 232–37; the evaluations by Jon Sobrino, Joseph Gremillion, and Robert McAfee Brown in *Puebla and Beyond*, ed. Eagleson and Scharper, 289–346; and Gutierrez, "Liberation and the Poor: The Puebla Perspective," in *The Power of the Poor in History*, trans. Robert R. Barr (Maryknoll, NY: Orbis, 1983) 125–65.

140. Dussel, in *Challenge of Basic Christian Communities*, ed. Torres and Eagleson, 97–98, and Dussel, *History of the Church in Latin America*, 237–39.

141. Lernoux, *Cry of the People*, 443–44.

of Nicaragua.[142] He became a symbol of liberation for Nicaragua when, in February 1934, Sandino was invited to dinner by the US supported leader, Anastosio Somoza Garcia (grandfather of Somoza Debyle); upon leaving the dinner, Sandino was murdered by Somoza's forces.[143] Since that time, the four pillars of Sandino's thought—nationalism, democracy, Christianity, and social justice—gave impetus to the revolutionary movements which finally led to the overthrow of the Somoza dictatorship.[144]

Of special significance was the role of Christianity and the church in the Nicaraguan revolution. In contrast to the Cuban revolution, many priests and Christian lay people took active part in the revolutionary process. For example, Father Ernesto Cardenal, together with many members of the Solentiname community, chose to take active part in the revolution.[145] Christians were also appointed as leaders in the new government, including Miguel d'Escoto as foreign minister and Ernesto Cardenal as minister of culture.[146]

At the meeting of the Ecumenical Association of Third World Theologians held in São Paulo in 1980, speakers from Nicaragua were given a significant place on the agenda. The liberation theologians present were influenced by the reports of recent events in Nicaragua. At this meeting Juan Hernandez Pico spoke optimistically of the compatibility between the Christian option for the poor and the project of socialism in Nicaragua. He attempted to minimize both Christian fear of atheistic ideology and mistrust of Christians by revolutionaries, speaking of the need for "a strategic alliance between non-believing revolutionaries and revolutionary Christians."[147] Miguel d'Escoto spoke of the hopes of the Nicaraguan people—their sense of paschal joy, their role as forgers of history, and

142. Joyce Hollyday and Jim Wallis, "Nicaragua: A Fragile Experiment," *Sojourners* 12.3 (1983) 8–10, and Blase Bonpane, "The Church in the Central American Revolution," *Thought* 59 (1984) 185–86.

143. Hollyday and Wallis, "Nicaragua," 9.

144. Miguel d'Escoto, "Nicaragua: An Unfinished Canvas—Building a New Nicaragua," *Sojourners* 12.3 (1983) 14–16.

145. Ernesto Cardenal, *The Gospel in Solentiname*, trans. Donald D. Walsh (Maryknoll, NY: Orbis, 1976) 1:267–71, and Ernesto Cardenal, "Nicaragua: A Priest in the Ministry," *Sojourners* 12.3 (1983) 22–23.

146. D'Escoto, "Nicaragua: An Unfinished Canvas," 18.

147. Juan Hernandez Pico, "The Experience of Nicaragua's Revolutionary Christians," in *The Challenge of Basic Christian Communities*, ed. Torres and Eagleson, 62–73 (quote on 72).

their solidarity in the revolutionary struggle.[148] Thus the revolution in Nicaragua became a symbol of the hope for liberation, reviving the idea of Christian participation in revolutionary activity at the end of a decade marked by an increase in repressive governments.

Among the most significant reforms by the new Nicaraguan government were its policies of land redistribution, rural development, and a gradual shifting from export to staple crops.[149] The Nicaraguan revolution was not without serious flaws, however. One of the most serious was the treatment of the Miskito Indians.[150] In admitting their mistakes in this regard, representatives of the Nicaraguan government have been strikingly candid.[151] Also, the Nicaraguan government was criticized for its censorship, the increasing militarization of the Nicaraguan society, and the delay of national elections. In the early 1980s the United States supported counterrevolutionary military forces based in Honduras and introduced strong economic sanctions against the Nicaraguan government. The US government justified these actions with reference to the failures of the Nicaraguan government in the areas of human rights and in delaying democratic elections. The desire to halt communism and defend US military and economic interests played a prominent role in the Central American policies of the US government.[152] At the same time a large number of US church leaders were highly critical of US policy, given evidence for their convictions by the reports of church representatives who visited Nicaragua.[153] The Nicaraguan revolution served as a symbol of hope for liberation theology in Latin America in the 1980s.

---

148. Miguel d'Escoto, "The Church Born of the People in Nicaragua," in ibid., 189–96.

149. John P. Olinger, "Land and Hunger: Nicaragua," *Bread for the World Background Paper* 71 (1983) 1–6.

150. Norman Bent, "Nicaragua: Bordering on Reconciliation," *Sojourners* 12.3 (1983) 24–28.

151. Hollyday and Wallis, "Nicaragua: A Fragile Experiment," 10, and Dan R. Ebener, "Is There a Future for Nonviolence in Central America?" *Fellowship* 49 (1983) 28.

152. See the reports appearing almost every week in *Time* magazine during 1982 and 1983 detailing new developments in US policy and activity regarding Nicaragua, for example, "Central America: The Big Stick Approach," *Time* 122.6 (1983) 6–13.

153. Jim Wallis and Joyce Hollyday, "A Plea from the Heart," *Sojourners* 12.3 (1983) 3–5, and Ebener, "Is There a Future for Nonviolence in Central America?" 6, 28.

The Vitality of Liberation Theology

THE DECADE OF THE 1980s

The 1980s were a decade of dramatic developments in the history of liberation theology. A major publishing project was initiated in 1985, a proposed fifty-volume collection of books to be known as the *Theology and Liberation Series*. Eleven volumes in the series were published between 1986 and 1988. These were also translated into English and published by Orbis Books. However, the combination of market pressures and increasing opposition by the Vatican led to the suspension of the series after the publication of only twelve of the projected books. Another major project, edited by Jon Sobrino and Ignacio Ellacuría and published as *Mysterium Liberationis: Fundamental Concepts of Liberation Theology*, encompassed fifty chapters.[154] This volume in many ways serves as the epitome in publishing by liberation theologians and remains a major milestone for all students in the field.

Due in part to interaction with theologians from other global contexts, the range of topics examined by Latin American theologians expanded in the 1980s, in particular in the areas of ecology and feminist theology. An increasing number of women liberation theologians began to participate in theological discussion, challenging liberation theology to incorporate a critique of sexism into its analysis.[155] The participation of Latin American theologians in EATWOT further contributed to the expansion of themes.

In the larger political landscape there was a shift away from government by dictatorship over the course of the decade with the shift to limited democracies in several countries. While the economic situation for the majority of the poor in Latin America remained in crisis, international pressures increased for Latin American governments to conform to free market standards, as established by international monetary organizations. The Reagan administration in particular implemented measures to pressure Third World governments to enact free market economic mechanisms that increased dependency on foreign investments and indebtedness to foreign banks.[156]

---

154. Iganacio Ellacuría and Jon Sobrino, eds., *Mysterium Liberationis: Fundamental Concepts of Liberation Theology* (Maryknoll, NY: Orbis, 1993).

155. For example, Elsa Tamez, ed., *Through Her Eyes: Women's Theology from Latin America* (Maryknoll, NY: Orbis, 1989).

156. Tombs, *Latin American Liberation Theology*, 204.

Emergence and Development of Liberation Theology

As part of the contest with the Soviet Union for global influence, the United States also exercised military force to stem the tide of communist influence, particularly in the Central American countries of El Salvador, Guatemala, and Nicaragua. In El Salvador internal pressures for more equitable distribution of wealth were opposed by the US-backed government, leading to a devastating civil war against guerrilla groups and their suspected sympathizers. The murder of six Jesuits (including Ellacuría), their housekeeper, and her daughter in November 1989 has been remembered as a particularly brutal act of violence against the church. In Nicaragua the US government supported the insurgency of the "contras" from military bases in Honduras in order to overthrow the Sandinista regime. In Guatemala massive state violence against the Mayan peoples aimed to defend the political and economic status quo by eliminating dissent. In other Latin American countries torture was used by the government to stifle opposition (for example, Chile[157]) and counterinsurgency against guerilla movements led to the terrorizing of civilian populations (for example, Peru).

US intelligence identified liberation theology as a particular threat to US business interests in Latin America, and steps were taken in the 1980s to undermine its influence. The Institute for Religion and Democracy was founded in 1981 as an independent organization which engaged in an ideological contest with liberation theology and has close ties with the US government. In a similar way the American Enterprise Institute supported a series of publications critical of liberation theology, especially research by and books authored by Michael Novak.[158]

Of chief importance for the future of liberation theology was the increasing opposition expressed by the Vatican under the leadership of John Paul II, especially as directed by Cardinal Joseph Ratzinger, who was appointed as prefect of the Congregation for the Doctrine of Faith in 1981. Throughout the decade of the 1980s, the Vatican engaged in a sustained effort to oppose the influence of liberation theology, particularly what were understood to be its most radical elements. The work of organizations like Opus Dei was strengthened and served as a counterforce to the proliferation of the liberation perspective. As new bishops

---

157. William T. Cavanaugh, *Torture and Eucharist: Theology, Politics, and the Body of Christ* (Malden, MA: Blackwell, 1998).

158. Craig L. Nessan, *Orthopraxis or Heresy: The North American Theological Response to Latin American Liberation Theology* (Atlanta: Scholars, 1989) 238–49.

were appointed, there was a consistent pattern of appointing those who opposed liberation theology. Cumulatively, this did much to stem the expansion of the base Christian community movement, which lost its connection to the institutional Roman Catholic Church.

The Vatican contested the appointment of priests as members of the Sandinista government in Nicaragua, leading to the suspension of four priests from the priesthood in January 1985.[159] Also during the 1980s, the Vatican undertook formal investigations of major liberation theologians, including Jon Sobrino, Gustavo Gutiérrez, and Leonardo Boff. The case against Boff involved an extensive investigation of his theology, particularly of his criticisms against the institutional church, and resulted in his silencing for a period of nearly a year.[160] During the period in which the writings of these major liberation theologians were being examined, two major critiques of liberation theology were issued by the Vatican: *Instruction on Certain Aspects of Liberation Theology*[161] (1984) and *Instruction on Christian Freedom and Liberation*[162] (1986). The use of Marxist categories in theological work, an overly politicized concept of liberation, and the advocacy of revolutionary violence as a means of social change received major criticism in these documents. While affirming the need for justice for the poor and a nuanced use of the idea of liberation, both documents advocated a more spiritual understanding of salvation from sin and defended the traditional sacramental ministry of the church. While the second instruction expressed a more positive appreciation for the theme of liberation, the term was appropriated into more traditional conceptuality based on freedom from sin. In response to the Vatican criticisms of liberation theology, many liberation theologians refused to acknowledge that the criticisms accurately depicted their own thought and writings. Some sought to appropriate the more positive references in the instructions into their own work.

More than anything else it was the appointment of a series of more conservative bishops throughout Latin America—many of whom were opponents of liberation thought—that had the greatest effect on

---

159. Tombs, *Latin American Liberation Theology*, 233–34.

160. For a detailed account of the case against Boff, see Harvey Cox, *The Silencing of Leonardo Boff: The Vatican and the Future of World Christianity* (Oak Park, IL: Meyer Stone, 1988).

161. *Instruction on Certain Aspects of Liberation Theology* (Vatican City: 1984).

162. *Instruction on Christian Freedom and Liberation* (Vatican City: 1986).

interrupting the influence of liberation theology. The decade of the 1980s ended with a monumental and little anticipated event that had dramatic significance for the future of Latin American liberation theology: the end of the Soviet Union, symbolized by the fall of the Berlin Wall in 1989, and the collapse of the Eastern Bloc.[163] In Nicaragua the defeat of the Sandinista party in the elections of February 1990 symbolized the arrival of the new world order to Latin America. World historical events seemed to have overtaken the vision of liberation for a more just future in Latin America.

THE 1990s AND BEYOND

The triumph of global capitalism beginning in the 1990s created a dramatically different context for liberation theologians. Dramatic structural change in the direction of socialism seemed impossible in the new political and economic context. The framing of the international landscape shifted from a confrontation between East and West to the enormous disparity between North and South. While the need for social justice among the poor was as great as or greater than ever, advocating for structural change employing the previous arguments appeared futile. As a consequence many liberation theologians began giving primary energy to local and regional issues (for example, climate change and deforestation) rather than focusing on macroeconomic issues. One particular focus was opposition to the North American Free Trade Agreement (NAFTA), which was understood to increase the dependency the Latin American countries on the North, thereby negatively affecting the lives of the poor.

CELAM IV, meeting at Santo Domingo in 1992, offered the increased number of conservative bishops the occasion for consolidating opposition to the perspective of liberation theology. Unofficial advisors were carefully excluded from conference proceedings and the concluding document depends on traditional theological categories which are employed apart from a close connection to the Latin American context.[164] By contrast, the five-hundred-year anniversary of the arrival of Christopher Columbus in the Americas also in 1992 gave occasion for addressing the decimation of the native peoples by the European conquest. Theolo-

---

163. Tombs, *Latin American Liberation Theology*, 275.

164. Alfred T. Hennelly, ed., *Santo Domingo and Beyond* (Maryknoll, NY: Orbis, 1993).

gians were able to offer analysis of the failure of the church to defend the rights of the indigenous peoples from a liberation perspective. Gustavo Gutiérrez authored a major work on Las Casas as a significant contribution to historical memory of this event.[165]

The expanded influence of Pentecostalism in Latin American offered the poor an alternative to the viewpoint of liberation theology. While Pentecostalism received much of its support from churches in North America, some of which were decidedly against liberation theology, Pentecostal congregations with their emphasis on the Spirit's work in the lives of the people could easily become indigenized among the Latin American poor. The mutual support by members of the Pentecostal fellowship, including what was needed for basic human survival, offered a practical and concrete response to the poverty that liberation theology had also attempted to address. David Martin has argued that Pentecostalism helped Christians in Latin America, including many formerly involved in the base community movement, to adjust to the new economic and political realities after the end of the socialist era and the victory of global capitalism.[166]

Increasingly by the 1990s dramatic changes in the political order, economy, institutional church, and society had interrupted the earlier momentum of liberation theology. This led many commentators, particularly critics, to speak of the "end" of liberation theology or even its "death."[167] Another challenge involved the need for a new generation of liberation theologians, equipped to engage the changed context from a liberation perspective.

David Tombs has argued that the very concept of liberation had lost its currency in the changed global environment. Nevertheless, the achievements of liberation theology needed to be recognized and appreciated:

> Despite this, liberation theology leaves a potent legacy within theology. It highlighted the political significance of all theological work, questioned the value of intellectual study divorced from

---

165. Gustavo Gutiérrez, *Las Casas: In Search of the Poor of Jesus Christ*, trans. Robert R. Barr (Maryknoll, NY: Orbis, 1993).

166. David Martin, *Tongues of Fire: The Explosion of Protestantism in Latin America* (Oxford: Wiley-Blackwell, 1993).

167. Robert A. Sirico, "Faith and the Free Market in the Third World: Death Knell for Socialism and Liberation Theology?" *Religion and Liberty* 1 (1991): http://www.acton.org/publications/randl/rl_article_1.php.

action, stressed the value of dialogue with those beyond the academy, and identified the struggles of the poor and oppressed as a privileged epistemological *locus* for an engaged theology.[168]

Tombs stressed the shift in liberation theology over the decades from a highly political and economic understanding of liberation to an epistemological understanding of liberation which privileged the perspective of the poor for theology. In addition, liberation theology has brought to prominence for theology and the church many biblical texts that demonstrate God's concern for the poor and oppressed.

Rather than claiming the demise of liberation theology, an unfinished task is to examine the manifold ways Latin American liberation theology has altered the entire global theological and ecclesial scene. For example, the ways systematic theology itself has been changed by the contributions of liberation theologians remains to be examined and documented.[169] In this way the perspective of liberation theology should no longer be understood as an enclave within theology but a dimension of all contemporary theology.

In concluding this account of liberation theology's contributions to Latin American history, it is important to note how this history continues to unfold among the Latin American people. The primary actors in this history remain nameless in this account. It is important to emphasize the unwritten history which continues to unfold in the parishes and Christian communities of Latin America.

---

168. Tombs, *Latin American Liberation Theology*, 295.

169. See chapter 4, "Orthopraxis and Martyrdom: The Influence of Latin American Liberation Theology on Systematic Theology in Europe and North America," in *Liberating Lutheran Theology: Freedom for Justice and Solidarity in a Global Context*, Paul S. Chung, Ulrich Duchrow, and Craig L. Nessan (Minneapolis: Fortress, 2011) 53–67.

4

Reading the Bible through Liberation Eyes

Justice Trajectory and the Gospel of Luke

LIBERATION THEOLOGY DEVELOPED AND implemented a radical hermeneutic for reading the Holy Scripture. It begins with "the view from below." This means it reads the entire Bible from the perspective of how it speaks to the situation of the poor and oppressed of this world. Whereas much contemporary theology has been preoccupied with how the Bible makes sense to the highly educated people of our time, liberation theologians bring the stories of God's Word into the gatherings of *campesinos* and the urban poor, women and day laborers, to listen to how God speaks a word of hope into their circumstances. One of the most poignant instances of the liberation reading of Scripture took place at Solentiname in Nicaragua under the leadership of Ernesto Cardenal. In *The Gospel at Solentiname*, Cardenal introduced and fostered a method of Bible reading where the poor of the parish gathered around specific texts to ask questions about what God had to say to them. Inevitably, the Spirit enlivened their collective reading to address the conditions of poverty and need faced by these peasants.

This chapter begins with a discussion of how liberation theology discloses a justice trajectory within the biblical tradition that appeals for recognition among all those who value the authority of Scripture. This justice trajectory runs in the Bible from the exodus in Egypt through the Christian Gospels to the book of Revelation. Secondly, this chapter takes a particular look at the Gospel of Luke, a book which is especially conducive to a liberating reading as Jesus is revealed as the friend of the poor and defender of the hungry. Thirdly, we will do a sociological analysis of the background behind the formation of Luke's Gospel. Through this procedure, we will discover that the Bible as a whole and individual books, including their sociological underpinnings, have much to contribute to opening our eyes to the God of justice who defends the poor and sends the rich away empty.

THE BIBLICAL IMPERATIVE OF JUSTICE

The call for justice permeates the witness of Scripture. God was revealed to Moses and the Israelites as a God of justice: "Then the Lord said: 'I have observed the misery of my people who are in Egypt; I have heard their cry on account of their taskmasters. Indeed, I know their sufferings, and have come down to deliver them from the Egyptians, and to bring them up out of that land to a good and broad land, a land flowing with milk and honey...'" (Exod 3:7-8; cf. also 2:23-25). The Lord hears the cries of the poor. In the promised land, there will be milk and honey, food for all.

One peculiar feature of the law codes of Israel was its insistence on justice. Because God is righteous, God's law insisted that the covenant people be a people of righteousness toward the most vulnerable in its midst: "For the Lord your God is God of gods and Lord of lords, the great God, mighty and awesome, who is not partial and takes no bribe, who executes justice for the orphan and the widow, and who loves strangers, providing them food and clothing" (Deut 10:17-18; cf. also 24:17-22). God's law made imperative the care for the least.

Leaders in Israel were expected to uphold a high standard of justice. Judges were expected to judge righteously. The king of Israel was expected to be the chief representative of God's justice: "So David reigned over all Israel; and David administered justice and equity to all his people" (2 Sam 8:15). Likewise with regard to Solomon: "Blessed be the Lord your God, who has delighted in you and set you on the throne of Israel! Because the Lord loved Israel forever, he has made you king to execute justice and righteousness" (1 Kgs 10:9). The Psalms resound with songs imploring God to make Israel's king just: "Give the king your justice, O God, and your righteousness to a king's son. May he judge your people with righteousness, and your poor with justice ... May he defend the cause of the poor of the people, give deliverance to the needy and crush the oppressor" (Ps 72:1-2, 4). The king is held to this standard because God is a God "who executes justice for the oppressed; who gives food to the hungry" (Ps 146:7). Jesus will draw from this royal tradition when he later announces the coming of God's kingdom.

Because the potential was so great for the king to abuse power out of self-interest, there emerged at the same time as the office of king another figure, the prophet, to offer a check on the abuse of royal authority. Perhaps nowhere in Scripture does God's word on behalf of the poor and hungry sound more clearly than in the oracles of these prophets: "He has told you, O mortal, what is good; and what does the Lord require of you but to do justice, and to love kindness, and to walk humbly with your God?" (Mic 6:8). Furthermore, Micah declares: "Hear this, you rulers of the house of Jacob and chiefs of the house of Israel, who abhor justice and pervert all equity, who build Zion with blood and Jerusalem with wrong! Its rulers give judgment for a bribe, its priests teach for a price, its prophets give oracles for money; yet they lean upon the Lord and say, 'Surely the Lord is with us! No harm shall come upon us.' Therefore because of you Zion shall be plowed as a field; Jerusalem shall become a heap of ruins . . ." (3:9–12).

To give another example, Jeremiah spoke this word of God to the king of Judah: "Woe to him who builds his house by unrighteousness, and his upper rooms by injustice; who makes his neighbors work for nothing, and does not give them their wages . . . Are you a king because you compete in cedar? Did not your father eat and drink and do justice and righteousness? Then it was well with him. He judged the cause of the poor and needy; then it was well. Is not this to know me? says the Lord" (Jer 22:13, 15–16).

When the Messiah would come, this one would finally rule as a just king, representing God's righteousness: "A root shall come out from the stump of Jesse, and a branch shall grow out of his roots. The spirit of the Lord shall rest on him, the spirit of wisdom and understanding, the spirit of counsel and might, the spirit of knowledge and the fear of the Lord. His delight shall be in the fear of the Lord. He shall not judge by what his eyes see, or decide by what his ears hear; but with righteousness he shall judge the poor, and decide with equity for the meek of the earth . . ." (Isa 11:1–4). Consistently throughout the Hebrew Bible, God is revealed as the one who executes justice for the poor and hungry and who requires those possessing political, social, and economic power to uphold this standard.

KINGDOM OF GOD, KINGDOM OF JUSTICE

When Jesus began his public ministry, he established his mission squarely within this justice trajectory: "The Spirit of the Lord is upon me, because he has anointed me to bring good news to the poor. He has sent me to proclaim release to the captives and recovery of sight to the blind, to let the oppressed go free, to proclaim the year of the Lord's favor" (Luke 4:18–19). At the center of Jesus' message was the proclamation of the kingdom of God. "Kingdom" is a political term—it was not an accident that Jesus selected this guiding image for his ministry—a term which summons forth Israel's hope for a just and righteous king in the face of oppression.[1]

Jesus drew upon the Hebrew Scripture's testimony to Yahweh as a just king and defender of the poor as he shaped his central image of the *basilea tou theou* (kingdom of God). The kingdom is not a place but the dynamic activity of God in the world now: "But if it is by the Spirit of God that I cast out demons, then the kingdom of God has come upon you" (Matt 12:28). "Once Jesus was asked by the Pharisees when the kingdom of God was coming, and he answered: 'The kingdom of God is not coming with things that can be observed; nor will they say, "Look, here it is!" or "There it is!" For, in fact, the kingdom of God is among you'" (Luke 17:20–21).

The kingdom Jesus proclaimed and instantiated brought the reign of God near to the people. Jesus' parables performed the kingdom,[2] invoking the arrival of a near and merciful God (cf. the parables of the Prodigal Son and the Good Samaritan). Jesus spoke pointedly on behalf of the hungry: "Blessed are you who are hungry now, for you will be filled... Woe to you who are full now, for you will be hungry" (Luke 6:21, 25). In the kingdom, the last will be first and the first last (Luke 13:30). In the parable of the rich fool, the rich man fails to see the folly of his ways and is unprepared for final judgment (Luke 12:16–21). Jesus summons the rich ruler to "sell all that you own and distribute the money to the poor," a form of repentance he is unwilling to undergo (Luke 18:18–25): "How hard it is for those who have wealth to enter the kingdom of God! Indeed, it is easier for a camel to go through the eye of a needle than for someone who is

---

1. Bruce Chilton, *Pure Kingdom* (Grand Rapids: Eerdmans, 1996) 23–44.

2. Norman Perrin, *Jesus and the Language of the Kingdom: Symbol and Metaphor in New Testament Interpretation* (Philadelphia: Fortress, 1976).

rich to enter the kingdom of God." Zacchaeus demonstrates, however, that with God all things are possible, even surrendering one's possessions to the poor (Luke 19:1-10). Jesus declares in response to Zacchaeus's act of relinquishment: "Today salvation has come to this house" (Luke 19:9).

Moreover, by his actions, Jesus instantiated the kingdom, that is, brought it into existence. Jesus healed the sick, cast forth demons, and miraculously fed hungry multitudes (Mark 6:30-44; 8:1-10). Jesus showed compassion for the crowds and challenged the disciples to respond in kind: "You give them something to eat" (Mark 6:37).

Jesus' own ministry was characterized particularly by unconventional table fellowship: "Why does he eat with tax collectors and sinners?" (Mark 2:16). The meals Jesus shared with others were a sign of the kingdom's in-breaking. He warned those who held banquets: "When you give a luncheon or a dinner, do not invite your friends or your brothers or your relatives or rich neighbors, in case they may invite you in return, and you would be repaid. But when you give a banquet, invite the poor, the crippled, the lame, and the blind" (Luke 14:12-13). Jesus poignantly depicted the anti-kingdom through the parable of the Rich Man and Lazarus (Luke 16:19-31). Consistent with his concern for the manifestation of the kingdom at table, Jesus left his disciples a simple meal by which to remember him: "While they were eating, he took a loaf of bread, and after blessing it he broke it, gave it to them, and said, 'Take; this is my body.'" Jesus' eating with tax collectors and sinners provides the framework for all eating at the Lord's Table: a welcome invitation to all, beginning with the outcast and sinners, the least. All are fed at the meal of Jesus.

The risen Jesus appeared to the disciples in the breaking of bread (Luke 24:30-31; cf. also John 21:12-13). The apostolic church of Acts is remembered for its generosity, which flowed out from its table fellowship: "All who believed were together and had all things in common; they would sell their possessions and goods and distribute the proceeds to all, as any had need. Day by day, as they spent much time together in the temple, they broke bread at home and ate their food with glad and generous hearts . . ." (Acts 2:44-46). In this regard, it is important to recall the original reason the church began to collect an offering: as a collection for the poor.[3] Likewise these early Christians remembered Jesus' words:

---

3. Gordon Lathrop, "Go in Peace, Remember the Poor: The Public Implications of the Eucharistic Setting," lecture given at the Institute on Liturgical Studies, Valparaiso University, Valparaiso, Indiana, April 1, 2008.

"... for I was hungry and you gave me food ... just as you did it to one of the least of these who are members of my family, you did it to me" (Matt 25:35, 40).

Jesus, as demonstrated by his unconventional table fellowship and his concentration on the coming of the kingdom, stands directly in the center of the Jewish justice tradition. Concern for food and the hungry belongs to the heart of Christian commitment. The church must read the Scripture as a summons to act with justice in service and advocacy on behalf of the poor.

SOCIOLOGY AND THE GOSPEL OF LUKE

Next we turn to an examination of the sociological background informing the Gospel of Luke, one of the most significant books for liberation theologians. The most prominent text from Luke which provides orientation for liberation theology is Jesus' appearance at his hometown synagogue in Nazareth to read from the Isaiah scroll. This text serves, in the eyes of liberation theologians, as a programmatic statement for the content of Jesus' ministry: to bring good news to the poor, release to the captives, recovery of sight to the blind, freedom for the oppressed, and the proclamation of the year of the Lord's favor (Luke 4:15–19). This final reference to "the year of the Lord's favor" is usually identified by liberation theologians with the Jubilee year, when by design debts would be cancelled and economic bondage overcome.[4] The entire agenda of Luke 4:18–19 is claimed as Jesus' own mission as he declares, "Today this scripture has been fulfilled in your hearing" (4:21). Such a political-economic program would prove itself radical not only within the context of the first century but just as much today. It's the sort of agenda that might get one crucified.

We will pursue two related lines of argument. First, we will examine Jesus' teachings on poverty and riches according to the testimony of Luke. Decisive for this task is an understanding of the socioeconomic circumstances of first-century Palestine in order to place the teachings of Jesus in their proper historical frame of reference. Second, we will argue that the radicality of Jesus' teachings were softened already within the narrative of Luke's Gospel insofar as Luke's message becomes one of exhorting wealthy Christians to be benevolent and generous to the poor, whereas

---

4. See Sharon H. Ringe, *Jesus, Liberation, and the Biblical Jubilee* (Philadelphia: Fortress, 1985).

the position of Jesus summons forth something far more exacting. Such a domestication of the message of Jesus is the constant temptation, not only in Luke but of all approaches based on literary criticism insofar as the presuppositions of the present situation become the filter through which the teachings of Jesus are strained. This means that a literary approach to the Bible requires grounding in historical-critical interpretation, lest the particularity and radicality of the incarnation of God in Jesus of Nazareth in first-century Galilee be compromised. To put the matter provocatively: the story of Jesus told apart from the social, economic, political, and religious context of first-century Galilee becomes docetic.[5]

VILLAGE ECONOMY AND THE PATRONAGE SYSTEM

Halvor Moxnes argues that "in antiquity the political and the economic systems were inseparable."[6] Furthermore, religion was fully embedded in the fabric of the single political-economic nexus. This means there was neither a doctrine of the two kingdoms nor a separation of church and state. What Jesus said religiously about poverty and wealth had very direct political and economic implications.

The basic political question in first-century Palestine was one of economic power: who controls the land and is in a position to profit from its productivity? For all practical purposes, there existed only two classes of people, a relatively small number (ca. 10 percent) of wealthy landowners and a large number (ca. 90 percent) of peasants who depend on the owners for their sustenance. The moral expectation placed upon the privileged minority was to deal generously with the peasant poor.[7] To this end, there evolved a patronage system between "patrons" and "clients" based on reciprocity: peasants devote themselves to work and loyalty to a patron in return for sustenance and generosity toward the peasants.

On a large scale, the Roman Empire was established as the highest center of authority which claimed the right to exact wealth from its provinces by means of taxes. On a smaller scale, local elites used their positions of power to administer the law, collect taxes, maintain civil order,

---

5. For example, Jack Dean Kingsbury, *Conflict in Luke: Jesus, Authorities, Disciples* (Minneapolis: Fortress, 1991) disregards the centrality of wealth-poverty as a conflicted issue in Luke.

6. Halvor Moxnes, *The Economy of the Kingdom: Social Conflict and Economic Relations in Luke's Gospel* (Philadelphia: Fortress, 1988) 27.

7. Ibid., 36–42.

distribute goods, and maintain their link to Roman rule.⁸ The analogies between the economic structure of first-century Palestine and the traditional economies of Latin America are striking.

Protest against the prevailing patronage system typically took place in one of two forms: (1) banditry, in which a strong leader bands together followers who live as "parasites" from the intact patronage system, or (2) a charismatic leader organized followers into an alternative community. Both forms of protest had minimal effect in changing the society as a whole.

The setting of Jesus' ministry in Luke's Gospel is primarily that of Galilean villages, with only its culmination in the city of Jerusalem. Villages in first-century Palestine were characterized by their small size, homogeneity of population, and total self-sufficiency. Villagers knew only the reality of their own village life and the proximate area around it. Moxnes characterizes the people of the village in Luke's Gospel according to three categories: (l) those on the periphery (the sick, the outcast, and the poor); (2) Jesus and his followers; and (3) the local leaders (elders, rulers, and sometimes Pharisees)."⁹ Wealth in villages derives from the land.¹⁰ The rich derive their wealth from farms, orchards, vineyards, and livestock. Peasants occupy a smaller parcel of land from which they attain their subsistence. Tenants are those with a yet greater dependency on landowners, to whom they were debtors because of their use of the land. Day laborers, servants, and slaves were virtually landless and precariously dependent upon employment by landowners. At the very margins of society were the widows, beggars, maimed, lame, blind, and bands of the poor. Local village leaders included judges, priests, Levites, and Pharisees. The entire village must itself be viewed as dependent upon regional political rulers and absentee landlords as well as the local landowners. The entire system is one of patronage between the powerfully wealthy and their clients. Luke refers frequently to debts and loans which indicate the pervasiveness of the patronage system.

For the peasant, life was lived according to constant scarcity. Life never afforded the accumulation of wealth but remained a matter of subsistence. Such economic realities lead to a fundamental conservatism, lest

---

8. Ibid., 44.
9. Ibid., 52–55.
10. Ibid., 57–60.

one's deviation from established patterns lead to the loss of subsistence. Peasants looked to wealthy patrons to provide for basic needs of housing, food, and clothing. In the case of food, one notices in Luke's gospel an awareness of the disparity between the full and the hungry (1:53; 6:21, 25; 16:19–21; 15:17). Basic diet consisted of bread and fish. Those with surplus food stood under a moral obligation to provide for hungry clients through patron-sponsored meals (cf. 15:3–10, 23). Those failing to employ their abundance to satisfy the needs of the hungry are held in contempt (12:16–21; 16:19–21). Food was to be "used for common consumption, for the benefit of everybody in the village, especially the needy."[11]

Luke's Gospel protests the neglect of the hungry by the rich within the context of the patronage system in the Galilean village. Religious leaders like the Pharisees are sharply criticized for their severity in matters of purity while neglecting the obligation to provide for the poor, for example, through almsgiving or redistributive table fellowship.

JESUS' RADICAL GOSPEL TO THE POOR

Virtually every chapter of Luke contains references to how Jesus carried out the programmatic agenda of 4:18–19 to "bring good news to the poor." When Jesus claims the text of Isaiah 61 as his own, Luke places him in continuity with both the ancient prophets who witnessed to God's requirement of justice for the poor and with Israel's messianic hopes for a Savior who would usher in the kingdom of ultimate justice.

One of the most difficult tasks of New Testament research is to sort out those traditions whose origins are most characteristic of the historical Jesus from those most probably accruing to the Jesus tradition at a later stage of development. This chapter follows the lead of scholars, such as John Dominic Crossan and especially Marcus Borg, in reconstructing the core teachings and ministry of Jesus of Nazareth.[12] One of the major criteria of authenticity is that of radicality, that is, the more radical the teaching about wealth and poverty, the more likely it stems from Jesus without later domestication by the church. The most radical sayings regarding

---

11. Moxnes, *Economy of the Kingdom*, 90.

12. Marcus J. Borg, *Jesus—A New Vision: Spirit, Culture, and the Life of Discipleship* (San Francisco: Harper & Row, 1987), and John Dominic Crossan, *Jesus: A Revolutionary Biography* (San Francisco: Harper & Row, 1994).

riches and poverty anticipate an absolute reversal of status between rich and poor in the kingdom. "Blessed are you who are poor, for yours is the kingdom of God . . . But woe to you who are rich, for you have received your consolation. Woe to you who are full now, for you will be hungry" (6:20–25). Likewise, in the Magnificat, Mary sings about the God who "has filled the hungry with good things, and sent the rich away empty" (1:53).

The story of Lazarus and the rich man also demonstrates poignantly the theme of eschatological reversal (16:19–26). Moreover, the apothegm of 13:30 states the matter most provocatively: "Indeed, some are last who will be first, and some are first who will be last." Each of these passages, by virtue of their very radicality, deserves consideration as belonging to the most original layer of Jesus' material.[13] Moreover, when one employs these texts at the heart of the Bible's liberation trajectory, other texts are illuminated as well.

According to a broad consensus of New Testament scholarship, the central concern of Jesus in his teachings and ministry was the kingdom of God. What distinguished the teaching of Jesus about the kingdom from the message of other eschatological prophets was the manner in which Jesus summoned his hearers and disciples to live already in the present according to the standards of the kingdom.[14] Two central emphases regarding the kingdom, consistent with the eschatological reversal sayings, are (1) the message of good news to the poor and (2) criticism of the rich. When the disciples of John inquired of Jesus whether he is "the one who is to come," Jesus replies, "Go and tell John what you have seen and heard . . . the poor have good news brought to them" (7:20–22).

In Luke 14:13 Jesus reminded the banquet givers of the responsibility to welcome the poor and marginal to their dinners, making those meals into occasions not of honoring those equal to one's own status but occasions of genuine redistribution. Similarly, in the parable of the Great Banquet (14:16–24), the owner of the house—out of exasperation at the excuses of the propertied who refused the invitation—finally does the right thing by inviting those who cannot repay: the poor, the crippled, the blind, and the lame. The theme of reversal appears here again with a

---

13. The following are identified as the "oldest traditions of the Gospels" by Walter E. Pilgrim, *Good News to the Poor: Wealth and Poverty in Luke-Acts* (Minneapolis: Augsburg, 1981) 57–63.

14. Cf. Pilgrim, *Good News to the Poor*, 62–63.

fresh twist. There is, in addition, a growing consensus of scholarly opinion that the actual table fellowship as practiced by Jesus was marked by "open commensuality," that is, by a radical openness to sup with those normally excluded from decent society—outcasts, public sinners, and tax collectors.[15]

The corollary of Jesus' message of good news to the poor is his calling the rich to repentance. In the parable of the rich fool, the rich man never recognizes the folly of his ways and so, at the hour of reckoning, finds himself prepared to meet the eschatological reversal (12:16–21). Jesus summoned the rich ruler to "sell all that you own and distribute the money to the poor," a form of repentance he was unwilling to undergo (18:18–25). "How hard it is for those who have wealth to enter the kingdom of God! Indeed, it is easier for a camel to go through the eye of a needle than for someone who is rich to enter the kingdom of God" (18:24–25). Zacchaeus showed, however, that with God all things are possible, even restitution of possessions to the poor by a rich man (19:1–10). Notice Jesus' words in response to Zacchaeus' act of justice to the poor: "Today salvation has come to this house" (19:9).

Those who followed Jesus as disciples were summoned to enter the eschatological reality already in the present. The cost of discipleship upon entry into the Jesus movement was leaving all security behind.[16] Simon, James, and John "left everything" to follow Jesus (5:11). Similarly, Levi the tax collector "left everything, and followed him" (5:28). Jesus instructed his disciples: "Sell your possessions, and give alms . . . For where your treasure is, there your heart will be also" (12:33–34). Again Jesus said to would-be followers: "None of you can become my disciple if you do not give up your possessions" (14:33). Jesus and his disciples are characterized by their poverty (9:3, 58; 10:4). The willingness to become poor is the only thing the rich ruler lacked which prevented him from becoming Jesus' disciple (18:22–23).

There are strong reasons to conclude that Jesus' position on riches and poverty contributed decisively to his eventual arrest and crucifixion. If Moxnes is correct, Jesus' polemic against the Pharisees was aimed primarily at their hypocrisy in demanding ritual purity while neglecting weightier matters of justice. They imposed strict (and often costly) ritual

---

15. Crossan, *Jesus*, 66–70.

16. Gerd Theissen, *Sociology of Early Palestinian Christianity*, trans. John Bowden (Philadelphia: Fortress, 1978) 33ff.

obligations upon those who could little afford them, while themselves neglecting the giving of alms (11:37–41; 14:7–14). For this reason, the Pharisees are identified in 16:14 as "lovers of money." It is likely Jesus' criticism of the Pharisees for their portion with the rich lead many of them actively to seek his death.

Two other references suggest Jesus' radical critique of riches contributed to his eventual arrest and crucifixion. First, the saying of Jesus regarding the payment of taxes—"Render to Caesar the things that are Caesar's and to God the things that are God's" (20:25)—far from being a statement of submissiveness to Roman authority, appears to move in exactly the opposite direction: Give your ultimate loyalty not to the emperor but to God alone! Even if Jesus did not advocate non-payment of taxes, nonetheless the ultimate authority of King Caesar is undercut and subordinated to the rule of God. Secondly, Jesus' prophet-like action in "cleansing" the temple is recalled as the act of driving out "those who were selling things there" and is interpreted according to the words of Isaiah 56:7: "My house shall be a house of prayer." Jesus added the pointed accusation, however: "But you have made it a den of robbers" (19:45–46). Jesus' critique of those who oppress the poor is thus evident to the very end of his ministry. If this prophetic action were also accompanied by predictions of the temple's destruction (21:5–7)—perhaps not so much in apocalyptic terms but rather in the prophetic sense that God brings judgment upon those who oppress the poor—then the stage is set for Golgotha.

If the preceding arguments are sound, then Jesus' radical teachings about poverty and wealth form a trajectory running from his appearance at his hometown synagogue to the very end of his life. They are not peripheral to understanding what Jesus stood for. Instead, they belong to the very core of his message and praxis. Jesus taught an unconventional wisdom which turned upside down the wisdom of a world that identified riches with God's blessing.[17] Jesus, the Messiah and Savior, is the one who bears good news to the poor and sets economic captives free. The echoes from Third Isaiah (cf. 4:18–19; 19:46) establish Jesus as the inaugurator of the eschatological community whose ways are justice and salvation.

---

17. Borg, *Jesus—A New Vision*, 97–124.

The Vitality of Liberation Theology

Jesus as Benefactor in Luke's Gospel

Frederick W. Danker describes Luke's understanding of Jesus as one of "benefactor.[18] In analogy to the Hellenistic notion of public officials as benefactors of the pubic and consistent with the Galilean village patronage system, Jesus is depicted in Luke as the "benefactor of all benefactors."[19] While Luke preserves *in nuce* the most radical teachings of Jesus regarding the danger of riches and the message about good news to the poor in terms of an eschatological reversal, these teachings are at the same time reinterpreted for the new situation faced by Luke's own community. The patronage system remained intact, with its characteristic disparity between the rich few who control the land and the poor majority who are dependent upon wealthy patrons for sustenance. However, one thing has changed. Growing numbers of the wealthy also now embrace Christianity. In this new situation, "Luke does not make total abandonment a once-for-all mark of Christian discipleship. It belongs uniquely to the time of Jesus and to those called by him to discipleship."[20] For example, in 22:35-38, we have evidence of an emerging situation where purse, bag, and sword have now become legitimate trademarks of the Christian missionary.

Luke's concern was to inspire all Christians—and especially the wealthy—to deeds of charity and benevolence patterned after the model and teachings of Jesus, the universal Benefactor. Note, however, the shift in emphasis! Although the radical texts of eschatological reversal between poor and rich are preserved, they function differently within the context of Luke's community. The demand to "leave everything" and follow Jesus is relativized in favor of an appeal to the generosity of the rich. The Pharisees are exhorted to give alms (11:41). Other texts similarly highlight the virtue of almsgiving (12:33; 18:22). This emphasis is further extended in the book of Acts (Acts 3:1–11; 9:36–43; 10:2, 4, 31; 24:17).

The Lukan application of Jesus' teachings on wealth and poverty can be further elaborated as entailing the obligation to do good with one's wealth. One should lend without expectation of repayment (6:27–36). Those who give will have a blessing returned to them (6:37–38). To forgive

---

18. Frederick W. Danker, *Jesus and the New Age: A Commentary on St. Luke's Gospel* (Philadelphia: Fortress, 1988).

19. Frederick W. Danker, *Luke* (Philadelphia: Fortress, 1976) 6–17.

20. Pilgrim, *Good News to the* Poor, 101.

debts incurs loyalty from one's clients (7:40–43). In offering banquets, one has an obligation to feed the poor and not just those who can repay the honor (14:7–24). The ultimate example of benefaction is that of the Good Samaritan, who risks his security and gives his possessions to help a stranger (10:29–37). While the story of Zacchaeus highlights the radicalness of Jesus' fellowship in welcoming tax collectors, the outcome—while itself impressive—is that Zacchaeus gives only half of his possessions to the poor, not all of them (19:8). Such stories as the Good Samaritan and Zacchaeus function to inspire generosity and benevolence among the Christian community without the radical demand that disciples must themselves become poor.

In the Acts of the Apostles, Luke further demonstrated his ideal of Christian community. The earliest church in Jerusalem is remembered as a community where "they would sell their possessions and goods and distribute the proceeds to all, as any had need" (Acts 2:45). This model was held up as an example for later generations: "Now the whole group of those who believed were of one heart and soul, and no one claimed private ownership of any possessions, but everything they owned was held in common" (4:32). Ananias and Sapphira, who hold back from the common treasury, meet a disastrous end (5:1–11). Imagine how such a story functioned to commend generosity! Over the course of the book of Acts, however, the theme of wealth and poverty faded into the background.[21] The danger of wealth as an obstacle to participation in the community was set aside in favor of the challenge of including Gentiles.

Consistent between Luke and Acts is the question of who are insiders and who are outsiders in God's community. Jesus' radical teaching about the abandonment of wealth yielded to Luke's emphasis on the need for the rich to be generous, which in turn gave way to the question in Acts about including Gentiles in the church.

LIBERATION THEOLOGY: ON NOT DOMESTICATING THE DANGEROUS MEMORY OF JESUS

The Lukan emphasis on the need for wealthy Christians to respond to the poor with benevolence, generosity, and charity is as necessary today as it was at the end of the first century. Especially among the churches of the

---

21. James A. Bergquist, "'Good News to the Poor'—Why Does This Lucan Motif Appear to Run Dry in the Book of Acts?" *Trinity Seminary Review* 9 (1987) 18–27.

First World, we need to recognize how many poor neighbors lie beaten on the side of the road to whom we are called to minister. Among the four Gospels, Luke raises most pointedly the problem of wealth and the obligation to respond to our Benefactor, Jesus, with beneficence to those who are poor.

The limitation of the Lukan rendering of Jesus' teachings on poverty and wealth is that in reinterpreting them for a new context, the radicality of Jesus' call to discipleship was tamed. The unconventional wisdom of Jesus, that one cannot serve both God and riches (16:13), became transformed into the conventional wisdom that it is virtuous to give alms. Perhaps it is only to be expected that a church cannot be built upon such a radical foundation. If poverty would have remained a constitutive mark of the church (that is, were we to confess, in the words of the Nicene Creed, that "we believe in one holy catholic apostolic and *poor* church"), the number of disciples, then as now, might be few. Luke's account of Jesus' ministry has been extremely effective in bringing the gospel to the multitudes—rich and poor, Gentiles and Jesus.

At the same time, however, lost in Luke's interpretation of Jesus as Benefactor was a more acute sense of the inherent danger of wealth as a rival to God, a sense of the radicalness of Jesus' call to discipleship, and a sense of the urgency of the eschatological now. Liberation theology, arising in the context of massive poverty, hears the Lukan texts with an ear for the radicality of Jesus' first proclamation of the kingdom of God. Liberation theologians summon us to attend to the theme of eschatological reversal between rich and poor that occupies central place in the earliest Jesus' material. Lest we succumb to a domestication of Jesus' teachings, which pacifies us in complacency about our own generosity, liberation theology hearkens us back to the "dangerous" and "subversive" memory of Jesus, who took up the cause of the poor.[22]

The theology of liberation will not allow us to remain smug in our efforts at charity. Armed with texts that recall the subversiveness of Jesus' teachings about blessings to the poor and woe to the rich, advocates of liberation theology challenge us with the proposal about "God's preferential option for the poor."[23] They insist that given the reality of massive

---

22. Johann Baptist Metz, *Faith in History and Society: Toward a Practical Fundamental Theology*, trans. David Smith (New York: Seabury, 1980) 90f.

23. Gustavo Gutiérrez, *A Theology of Liberation: History, Politics, and Salvation*, trans. and ed. Caridad Inda and John Eagleson (Maryknoll: Orbis, 1988) xxv–xxviii.

starvation and unimaginable disparity between the rich and poor, mere charity is not enough. Alms, perhaps, serve mainly to appease our own tender consciences. Instead, radical structural adjustments are required in international banking policies and global economic systems. Such changes, requiring the redistribution of the world's wealth, may mean a lower standard of living for those profiting from the economic status quo. As interpreted by liberation theologians, the dangerous memory of the crucified Jesus threatens to once again turn the world upside down.

Supported by the texts preserved by Luke regarding wealth and poverty, liberation theology challenges us to incorporate within our understanding of salvation the dimension of justice for the oppressed. The Lukan Jesus stands in continuity with the exodus and the prophets in challenging oppressors with the demand that they surrender their privileges so the hungry may be fed. Even as we defend forgiveness of sins and eternal life as essential elements in the meaning of Christian salvation, liberation theologians make frequent reference to Luke in constructing a vision of God's shalom, which includes justice for the poor.[24]

While literary criticism has done much to enliven our imaginations by filling us with stories both biblical and contemporary, without serious historical grounding we can succumb to the tendency to deliver the gospel over to contemporary cultural forms. Luke faced this challenge as he told the story of Jesus for the next generation just as much as we may do so today. The perennial temptation is this: to interpret Jesus so as to accommodate his dangerous memory to our own conventional standards and values. Whenever that happens, we succumb to the lure of creating a docetic Christ that has little to do with Jesus of Nazareth. The scandal of the incarnation is that God became incarnate in this world in the flesh and blood of a particular human being: the Jesus who gave everything away, even life itself, to save the world. Liberation theology has done much to preserve the dangerous memory of Jesus and to deliver us from this temptation.

---

24. Craig L. Nessan, *Shalom Church: The Body of Christ as Ministering Community* (Minneapolis: Fortress, 2010), chapter 5.

5

Praxis

The Method of Liberation Theology

"Praxis" as a term has come to express a dramatic contrast between liberation theology and those forms of theology that take academia as their primary social location. Instead of beginning with the intellectual questions of the university context, liberation theology sees the reality of poverty as its social location and Latin American history as its theological starting point. Thereby liberation theologians have emphasized that this theology does not only attempt to understand the world but to change it (Karl Marx).[1] While Latin American liberation theologians have not shied away from a critical encounter with Marxist thought, which includes respect for Marx's strong emphasis upon praxis for the sake of social change, a careful consideration of what praxis means in the thought of particular liberation theologians reveals that their understanding of praxis can in no way be reduced to captivity to the philosophy of Karl Marx.[2]

This chapter argues that the idea of praxis among liberation theologians derives from a number of sources and not exclusively from Marx. Both the Latin American context of poverty (see chapter 1) and the biblical witness to justice (see chapter 4) are essential for a balanced understanding of what they mean by praxis. After initial reflections on praxis as constitutive for the very definition of liberation theology's method, we will turn to an exposition of the meaning of praxis in four different liberation theologians: Gustavo Gutiérrez, Juan Luis Segundo, José Porfiro Miranda, and José Míguez Bonino.

---

1. Cf. Karl Marx, "Theses on Feuerbach," http://www.marxists.org/archive/marx/works/1845/theses/index.htm, November 29, 2011, especially thesis 11.

2. See especially the *critical* analysis of Marxist thought by José Míguez Bonino, *Christians and Marxists: The Mutual Challenge to Revolution* (Grand Rapids: Eerdmans, 1976).

PRAXIS AS THE METHOD OF LIBERATION THEOLOGY

Praxis needs to be understood as nothing less than *the very method of liberation theology*. Praxis does not mean pure activism but a complex interaction involving biblical and theological reflection about concrete life experience in the Latin American context which is oriented toward social change. Five basic elements combine to constitute what liberation theologians mean when they speak of praxis.[3]

1. A living encounter with the social, political, economic, and religious context of Latin America.
2. An ethical moment of prophetic indignation at the extreme poverty and oppression in that context.
3. The application of social analysis to understand the causes of poverty and oppression, including a critical use of Marxist thought.
4. Biblical and theological reflection on Latin American experience.
5. Engagement for the change of unjust social structures.

Together these elements interact to create a theology which liberation theologians defend as both adequate to the biblical witness and imperative for their own historical context.[4]

It is important to stress both the Latin American and the biblical roots of liberation theology's understanding of praxis, especially in response to the attempts of critics to discredit the genuine gospel concern of liberation theology for the poor and oppressed people of Latin America by labeling Marxism as its primary source.[5] One would not turn to the thought of Marx to explain the Old Testament concern for the poor which culminated in the message of the prophets nor to explain the numerous texts in the gospels which articulate Jesus' own gospel of the kingdom for the poor and social outcasts of the first century. These, however, are the

---

3. Cf. Leonardo Boff, "Die Anliegen der Befreiungs-theologie," *Theologische Berichte* 8 (1979) 71–103, and Clodovis Boff, *Theologie und Praxis: Die erkenntnistheoretischen Grundlagen der Theologie der Befreiung* (Munich: Kaiser-Grunewald, 1983), for firsthand elaborations of the idea of praxis by Latin American liberation theologians.

4. For a fuller exposition, see Craig L. Nessan, *Orthopraxis or Heresy: The North American Theological Response to Latin American Liberation Theology* (Atlanta: Scholars, 1989) 65–121.

5. Cf. the criticisms by the Sacred Congregation for the Doctrine of the Faith, "Instruction on Certain Aspects of the 'Theology of Liberation,'" (Vatican City: Vatican Polyglott Press, 1984).

primary scriptural references which permeate the writings of the various liberation theologians. While a differentiated appeal to Marxist analysis has influenced liberation theology, this must be seen as one factor among several and not the decisive one. To dismiss as Marxist liberation theology's critique of the North's complicity in Latin American poverty ignores the powerful biblical and theological arguments developed by the liberation theologians themselves.

The praxis orientation of liberation theology expresses itself in differentiated ways among different Latin American liberation theologians. We will next examine the distinctive praxis orientation of four particular Latin American liberation theologians, in order to illustrate the concrete meaning of praxis in their respective theological writings.

GUSTAVO GUTIÉRREZ: THEOLOGY FOR THE POOR

The theology of Gustavo Gutiérrez is *a theology for the poor of Latin America*. He writes from the point of view of the poor, in solidarity with the poor, and for the sake of their liberation. It is in his concern for the poor and for challenging the powers which oppress them that Gutiérrez's theology reveals itself as one fully oriented toward praxis.

In every respect, the theology of Gutiérrez is oriented toward praxis in service to the poor. An excellent overview of his praxis orientation can be obtained from his collected essays from the years 1969–1979 under the title, *The Power of the Poor in History*. This volume demonstrates Gutiérrez's reflections upon biblical sources, the bishop conferences at Medellin and Puebla, and the state of modern theology. Each of these sources of authority is evaluated in terms of their impact upon the "poor of the earth." One should note the plenitude of biblical references and the paucity of references to Marx. It is *the poor* who are understood as the starting point for "a rereading of history."[6] The poor are those whom God has chosen to love "simply because they are poor, simply because they are literally and materially poor."[7] The poor are those through whom God works to

---

6. Gustavo Gutiérrez, *The Power of the Poor in History*, trans. Robert R. Barr (Maryknoll, NY: Orbis, 1983) 201.

7. Ibid., 95.

Praxis: The Method of Liberation Theology

"subvert" history.⁸ The poor are those who offer a virtually sacramental encounter with God.⁹

Also in his major work, *A Theology of Liberation*, the poor provide the axis around which the whole revolves. In Gutiérrez's very definition of theology, it is "commitment to the service of men [*sic*]" (in the Latin American context this means commitment to the poor) which is the first step after which theological reflection follows as a second step.¹⁰ His critique of the idea of development and support of the theory of dependency are based upon their impact on the poor. Gutiérrez's interpretation of the Bible is executed from the perspective of the poor. His criticism of other theological positions (as well as his own theological reformulations) are each thoroughly informed by the plight of the poor.

> Only authentic solidarity with the poor and a real protest against the poverty of our time can provide the concrete, vital context necessary for a theological discussion of poverty. The absence of sufficient commitment to the poor, the marginated, and the exploited is perhaps the fundamental reason why we have no solid contemporary reflection on the witness of poverty.¹¹

At every turn, Gutiérrez brings his central concern of praxis for the poor to the forefront.

It is not sufficient that theologians themselves begin to do theology from the point of view of the poor. While this would be a welcome change, something more is yet required.

> But in the last instance we will have an authentic theology of liberation only when the oppressed themselves can freely raise their voice and express themselves directly and creatively in society and in the heart of the People of God, when they themselves "account for the hope," which they bear, when they are the protagonist of their own liberation.¹²

---

8. Cf. ibid., 20–21, 105ff., 202.

9. See the comments of Robert McAfee Brown, "Preface: After Ten Years," in ibid., xiv.

10. Gustavo Gutiérrez, *A Theology of Liberation*, trans. and ed. Caridad Inda and John Eagleson (Maryknoll, NY: Orbis, 1973) 11.

11. Ibid., 302.

12. Ibid., 307.

The poor must themselves become the leading characters of their own future.

Gutiérrez has been at the forefront of raising the consciousness of the poor through his theological and pastoral work. Gutiérrez believes there has been growth in the *conscientization* of the poor, as witnessed in his explication of the spirituality of liberation theology in the book, *We Drink From Our Own Wells*. Here the reader is compelled to acknowledge that the arguments of Gutiérrez are steeped in biblical and theological sources.[13] Gutiérrez speaks of the poor as awakening to a new awareness of the identity *as followers of Jesus in their own context*.

> The breakthrough or irruption—as it has been called—of the poor in Latin America not only left its mark on the beginning of the theology of liberation but is daily becoming more urgent and massive, even where the effort is made to hide or repress it. This has simply reinforced the fact that the entrance of the poor onto center stage in Latin American society and the Latin American church has plowed new furrows for Christian life and reflection.[14]

The theological contributions of Gutiérrez express his central concern for the poor, a concern which leads consequently to commitment and involvement. Beginning with his fundamental option for the poor, the theology of Gutiérrez is oriented toward and rooted in praxis, the commitment to change the social structures which oppress the poor.

JUAN LUIS SEGUNDO: THEOLOGY FOR ARTISANS OF A NEW HUMANITY

The praxis orientation of Juan Luis Segundo is well expressed in the title which unites his five-volume work: *A Theology for Artisans of a New Humanity*. The format and origin of these contributions disclose his basic concern. They arose out of the context of a series of pastoral seminars which Segundo directed for laity. They demonstrate Segundo's response to what he perceived to be a crisis of faith.

> Those who "have the faith" often see it as something that *should be* the most dynamic and meaningful thing for living in today's

---

13. Cf. Robert McAfee Brown, "Drinking from Our Own Wells," *The Christian Century* 101 (1984) 483–86.

14. Gustavo Gutiérrez, *We Drink from Our Own Wells: The Spiritual Journey of a People*, trans. Matthew J. O'Connell (Maryknoll, NY: Orbis, 1984) 1–2.

> world. But in fact it is not. All too often it has been transformed into a hideout for people who dare not or cannot live the adventure of being *a human being today*.[15]

This text expresses Segundo's deep concern, one that is intimately related to praxis. He aims to spur on Christian faith to a new level of maturity, in order that this faith might be lived out in the present historical moment.

Segundo has theological reasons for wanting to develop a mature and faithful Christian laity. Influenced by Teilhard's evolutionary understanding of history, Segundo has from the time of his earliest writings interpreted Scripture, Christian doctrine, and history itself as being in a process of evolutionary development.[16] Thereby Segundo describes the Bible as "the education in faith of God's chosen people, provided by [God] in the different stages of that same education."[17] Christian doctrine is understood not as expressing timeless truths but rather is to be interpreted according to the levels of truth which have been progressively revealed over the course of history. Interpreting history plays a crucial role for Segundo as the present moment is understood in light of the history which has gone before and the future which lies ahead. The task of the present moment is to stimulate humanity to take the next evolutionary step in accordance with God's future.

In the ongoing process the church, the agency of the laity has a vital function. The church—not as an institution for the masses but rather as a creative minority—has an important role in stimulating human history toward its final goal. Segundo's understanding of the church needs to be interpreted in light of the evolutionary scope of his thought. Christ has given a creative impulse to history which is now carried forward by Christian minorities.

> . . .the triumph of love throughout the evolutionary process is never a quantitative one. It is a minority affair without being an elitist one. It is a minority affair because it wells up from the entropy-ridden base that continues to dominate quantitatively even on the human level. It is not elitist because the love which comes

---

15. Segundo, *The Community Called Church*, trans. John Drury (Maryknoll, NY: Orbis, 1973) vii.

16. Cf. Alfred T. Hennelly, *Theologies in Conflict: The Challenge of Juan Luis Segundo* (Maryknoll, NY: Orbis, 1979) 52ff., and especially Segundo's own book *Evolution and Guilt*, trans. John Drury (Maryknoll, NY: Orbis, 1974).

17. Segundo as quoted by Hennelly, *Theologies in Conflict*, 52.

> to life is at the service of negentropy in the universe. It structures the universe for syntheses that are richer, more human, more redemptive.[18]

For the advancement of human history, the church by demonstrating God's love carries out this catalytic task. Segundo's concern for a mature laity is grounded in his evolutionary understanding of God's work in history. The praxis of the laity is the criterion not only for the Christian faith itself but for the forward movement of human history.

This evolutionary understanding of history provides the hermeneutical key for the praxis orientation of Segundo. This lens also informs Segundo's reflections on the resistance of the institutional church to progressive change and his call for a new ecclesiology in his earlier work, *The Hidden Motives of Pastoral Action*.[19] Segundo's entire thought finds its interpretive framework by understanding the crucial role of the church in catalyzing the unfolding of universal history. Likewise, the hermeneutical method elaborated in *The Liberation of Theology* encompasses the scheme of evolutionary history in its argument.[20] Segundo's insistence upon social analysis, discussion of the inevitably ideological and political nature of human reality, critique of popular religion, and option for socialism are each proposed, in order that history might move toward its next stage. Segundo's fundamental model orients itself toward praxis for the sake of evolutionary history. The artisans of a new humanity, the primary interlocuters of his theology, are those who through their loving action and praxis will move history progressively closer to its final destiny in God.

JOSÉ PORFIRO MIRANDA: THE CONVERGENCES OF MARXISM AND THE BIBLE

The praxis orientation of José Porfiro Miranda, more pointedly than any other liberation theologian, focuses on the thought of Marx. His prevailing concern is to argue against those who assume an inherent contradiction between Marx and the Bible, asserting that in fact the two are compatible and even convergent. The point of convergence between Marx and the Bible, according to Miranda, is their common concern for human

---

18. Segundo, *Evolution and Guilt*, 113.

19. Juan Luis Segundo, *The Hidden Motives of Pastoral Action* (Maryknoll, NY: Orbis, 1978).

20. Juan Luis Segundo, *The Liberation of Theology* (Maryknoll, NY: Orbis, 1976).

justice. Miranda interprets both Marx and the biblical writings in order to emphasize social justice as their common concern. Social justice means the end of the exploitation of the poor and disadvantaged. This concept of justice, according to Miranda, is contradicted by the inherently exploitative nature of modern capitalism.

The praxis orientation of Miranda is inseparable from his use of a Marxist analysis of Western society. Miranda's *Marx and the Bible* begins with a sharp critique of the capitalist underpinnings of Western society.[21] This critique, based on Marxist constructs, provides the hermeneutical key for understanding Miranda's interpretation of the Bible. Like Marx, Miranda analyzes how the capitalist economic system by its very nature results in the impoverishment of the masses. Accordingly, it is not surprising that Miranda also arrives at conclusions which echo Marx's call for revolution.

What is surprising is the elaborate exegesis which Miranda employs to make his case for rereading the Bible through the angle of historical materialism. Whereas both Old and New Testaments have been subject to interpretations which avoid, if not deny, their rootedness in justice on this earth, Miranda interpretation of the Bible begins and ends with this concern. The prohibition against divine images, knowledge of Yahweh, Israelite cult, Exodus, prophets, law, gospels, and Pauline theology are each given fresh meaning through Miranda's interpretation, which prompts the reader to reaccess the theological significance of the biblical concern for human justice. It is not necessary to agree with Miranda regarding every exegetical decision to be awakened to the Bible's overwhelming concern for interhuman justice. This is also true for his commentary on the Gospel of John, *Being and the Messiah*.[22]

Miranda's *Communism in the Bible* provides a concise summary of his program, which he names a "manifesto."[23] Although never afraid of controversy, in this slim volume Miranda states his case to provoke a response.

> This is a manifesto. But it is a biblical manifesto, which submits to all the rigor of scientific exegesis and accepts its challenge . . .

---

21. José Porfirio Miranda, *Marx and the Bible* (Maryknoll, NY: Orbis, 1974).

22. José Porfirio Miranda, *Being and the Messiah* (Maryknoll, NY: Orbis, 1977).

23. José Porfirio Miranda, *Communism in the Bible*, trans. Robert R. Barr (Maryknoll, NY: Orbis, 1982) ix.

> Precisely what this book recriminates in official theology is the lubrication of a whole concept of Christianity independently of the Bible and even in contradiction to it.[24]

Starting with this assertion, Miranda presents and defends the thesis that Christianity itself is a form of communism.[25] Clearly by "communism" he does not mean any of its contemporary forms. Rather, he aims to dispel the notion that a Christian can "claim to be anti-Communist."[26]

Based on texts drawn chiefly from the gospels and Acts, Miranda defends the thesis that the character of Jesus' proclamation of the kingdom and the earliest Christian community should be understood materially. Miranda introduces many biblical texts to demonstrate how the Bible attacks wealth and riches due to their origin in the practice of injustice.[27]

> The biblical reprobation of differentiating wealth is cohesive and without loopholes. The attack is not only against wealth already acquired and established, but also on the sole means by which wealth came to be, which is the taking of profit; and it is not only against profit in general, but also on the various kinds of profit—each and every one of the methods that can exist for acquiring profit in an economic system. With what conscience before God the theologians have been able to evade this absolutely central message of the Bible is beyond my comprehension. If we want to know "Why communism?" the response is unequivocal: because any other system *consists* in the exploitation of some persons by others. Just because of that.[28]

The weaving together of Marx with biblical texts leads Miranda to this provocative conclusion regarding the necessity of an economic system based on the principles of communism.

Miranda presents the most radically Marxist position among all liberation theologians. Nevertheless, his biblical scholarship does not allow his arguments to be dismissed for this reason. Although he does not detail the course of action to be followed, the praxis orientation of his thought is crystal clear. The Bible, consistent with the fundamental concern of Marx, requires the exercise of social justice. Only those who do justice have any

---

24. Ibid.
25. Cf. Porfiro Miranda, *Communism in the Bible*, 1–7
26. Ibid., 1.
27. See ibid., 30–56.
28. Ibid., 55.

Praxis: The Method of Liberation Theology

claim to the knowledge of God because, in biblical terms, the two are identical.[29] The Bible directs Christians to commit themselves to the pursuit of justice and the advocacy of a new system based on the principles of "communism." Moreover, violence cannot be eliminated as a means to this end. When one grasps the basic shape of Miranda's thought from the viewpoint of the oppressed, there is no mistake about their implications for praxis. Revolution is required in order that a system more in accord with God's way of justice might be created.

JOSÉ MÍGUEZ BONINO: AT THE INTERFACE OF THEOLOGY AND ETHICS

In the preface to *Christians and Marxists*, José Míguez Bonino writes about his own understanding of the book:

> This author is neither a politician nor a sociologist. He is a theologian trying to discharge his political responsibility as theologian, which means at the theoretical level that corresponds to academic work, with all its dangers and frustrations. But, to the extent that the position taken in this book is correct, such work can only have meaning if it faithfully assumes, in the light of the Gospel, the real commitment of Christians and offers a possibility of deepening, correcting, and strengthening such commitment.[30]

This citation serves as an interpretive key to the entire theological program of Miguez Bonino. His understands his work as a theologian to be directly connected to political responsibility and practical Christian commitment. In short, Miguez Bonino carries out his task at the interface where theology and ethics meet. In this way his praxis orientation becomes manifest.

Míguez Bonino focuses on the ethical implications of theology. In *Christians and Marxists*, he subjects Marxist thought to critical examination on the basis of Christian principles. He explains how Christians have been attracted to Marxist thought due to their concern for a faith which is relevant to the challenges of the Latin American context. In critically appraising Marxism from a Christian viewpoint, Miguez Bonino demonstrates his concern for a relevant faith and highlights the ethical issues

---

29. See José Porfiro Miranda, *Marx and the Bible: A Critique of the Philosophy of Oppression*, trans. John Drury (Maryknoll, NY: Orbis, 1974) 44–53.

30. Míguez Bonino, *Christians and Marxists*, 10.

which arise as a result of Christianity's encounter with Marxism. He offers no blanket endorsement of Marxism, but rather measures Marxism on the scales of Christian ethics.[31]

Another ethical issue of interest to Míguez Bonino is the use of violence by Christians as a means of social change.[32] In seeking a balanced approach, he considers a definition of violence that is specific to the Latin American context and the Christian ethical criteria which are pertinent to the issue. Míguez Bonino combines his theological concern with ethics, in order to address Latin American praxis.

In *Toward a Christian Political Ethics*, which collects the accumulated wisdom of years of struggling with theological-ethical questions, Míguez Bonino addresses two particular groups: Christians involved in politics and those involved in ecumenical work. This twofold audience demonstrates Míguez Bonino's interest both in concrete Latin American praxis and in serving as a spokesman to an international audience. The book deals with issues dear to Míguez Bonino's heart: the need for Christians to develop political ethics, engage in social analysis for the sake of praxis, and employ their faith to articulate theological principles to guide ethical deliberation. Two chapters are devoted to the Latin American context. Míguez Bonino never develops his ethical ideas in the abstract; the Latin American context remains his constant point of reference.

Two short excerpts demonstrate how Miguez Bonino places theology in the service of ethics. The first defends the rights of the poor as a fundamental ethical criterion for theology:

> The true question is not "what degree of justice (liberation of the poor) is compatible with the maintenance of the existing order?" but *"What kind of order is compatible with the exercise of justice (the right of the poor)?"* Here alone do we find an adequate point of departure for the theological determination of priorities.[33]

---

31. Míguez Bonino, *Christians and Marxists*, 130–32.

32. See José Míguez Bonino, "Violence & Liberation," *Christianity & Crisis* 32 (1972) 169–72, and "Violence: A Theological Reflection," in *Third World Theologies*, ed. Gerald H. Anderson and Thomas F. Stransky (New York: Paulist, 1976) 118–26.

33. José Míguez Bonino, *Toward a Christian Political Ethics* (Philadelphia: Fortress, 1983) 86. See also the essays "The Struggle of the Poor and the Church," *Ecumenical Review* 27 (1975) 36–43; "Poverty as Curse, Blessing and Challenge," *Iliff Review* 34 (1977) 3–13; and "Doing Theology in the Context of the Struggles of the Poor," *Mid-Stream* 20 (1981) 369–73, for the ways poverty has been a determinative factor in the work of Míguez Bonino.

Praxis: The Method of Liberation Theology

Míguez Bonino insists on justice for the poor not as one ethical criterion among many but as the starting point and exclusive criterion for ethics from a theological perspective. Another interconnected issue received prominent attention in the later writings of Míguez Bonino: the basic affirmation of the humanity of the poor.

> When we speak about a project of liberation, we are talking about persons—about irreplaceable human subjects, unique human faces.[34]

In stating this fundamental truth, Míguez Bonino restores to ethics its ultimate criterion, that persons are to be valued more than things and treated as precious creatures of God. Theological ethics arises out of the most basic of Christian motives: the love of God in Christ.

According to Beatriz Melano Couch, Míguez Bonino "is the ethicist of the Protestant reflection on liberation."[35] In his insistence that theology fulfill itself in ethical reflection and practice, Míguez Bonino contributes to the praxis orientation of liberation theology. His unique blend of theological and ethical insights, oriented toward praxis, come to full expression in his conclusion of *Toward a Christian Political Ethics*:

> The resurrection comes not to cancel out the cross, not to ensure a visible victory, but rather to confirm Jesus' praxis of love and justice and thus to incite a participation in that praxis, in the sure hope that such praxis is not lost but always recovered and incorporated in the future of the kingdom. The power of death is not magically suspended, but the praxis of vicarious love ("laying down our life for the brethren") through death reaches its final consummation. This is not merely an assertion about the triumph of a cause, but the confession of a faith in the historical and eternal vindication of innocent suffering and committed love (and of those who personally bear them). Confident following is the correlate of the Cross.[36]

---

34. Míguez Bonino, *Toward a Christian Political Ethics*, 111. See also the book *Room to Be People: An Interpretation of the Bible for Today's World*, trans. Vickie Leach (Philadelphia: Fortress, 1979), and the article "The Human and the System," *Theology Today* 35 (1978) 14–24, on the value of the human for theology and ethics.

35. Beatriz Melano Couch, "New Visions of the Church in Latin America: A Protestant View," in *The Emergent Gospel: Theology from the Developing World*, ed. Sergio Torres and Virginia Fabella (London: Chapman, 1978) 214.

36. Míguez Bonino, *Toward a Christian Political Ethics*, 115.

The Vitality of Liberation Theology

For Míguez Bonino, Christian faith and theology meet the ethical challenges of the Latin American context and creatively combine in a way which undergirds and promotes active engagement in praxis.

THE CHALLENGE OF LIBERATION PRAXIS TO LUTHERAN THEOLOGY

This chapter contends that praxis must be understood as nothing other than the very method of liberation theology. Attempts to reduce the understanding of praxis in liberation theology to the Marxist concept are inadequate. This examination of the meaning of praxis in four Latin American liberation theologians demonstrates complexity which defies blanket generalizations. While the thought of Marx may be referenced in these theologies, what decisively shapes the notion of praxis comes primarily from biblical and theological resources. For Gutiérrez the Latin American context of the poor is decisive, especially in conjunction with biblical passages which advocate for the poor. For Segundo it is the Teilhardian idea of God's evolutionary history which plays the leading role in defining praxis as that which spurs history forward. Of the four liberation theologians here examined, only Miranda's thought can be judged as decisively influenced by Marx. Yet even here his exegesis demands consideration on its own merit. For Míguez Bonino, the paradigmatically Protestant movement from theology to ethics, gospel to works, and faith to love is decisive in shaping his understanding of praxis.

Contrary to the varied critics, liberation theology is finally a theology deeply motivated by the gospel.[37] This gospel motivation may be left implicit too often to suit conventional standards of orthodoxy. For example, the distinction between law and gospel may not be sufficiently articulated. But there are decidedly historical reasons for such theological differences. This theology has arisen in an historical context markedly different from Germany in the sixteenth century. Theologians who watch thousands die daily from hunger and its correlates rightly have a different theological agenda from Luther in his context. In the contemporary context of hungry people, the gospel of Jesus Christ must speak of good news to the poor, release to the captives, liberty for the oppressed, and

---

37. Cf. Carl E. Braaten, "Praxis: The Trojan Horse of Liberation Theology," *Dialog* 23 (1984) 276–80.

Praxis: The Method of Liberation Theology

the coming of the acceptable year of the Lord (Luke 4:18–19), all solidly grounded in the proclamation of Jesus.

Jesus' gospel of the kingdom has rightly been understood by scholars as the proclamation of the coming of God's eschatological kingdom. But this kingdom itself entails a definite content which includes interhuman justice. As we wait for the eschatological arrival of God's kingdom, it is imperative that Christians seek to embody that kingdom already in the present in their personal and social lives, even if only in a fragmentary approximation of the final kingdom. It is from this gospel vision of the kingdom of God that liberation theology grounds its insistence on praxis.[38] This gospel message is deeply grounded both in the prophets of the Hebrew Bible and in the teachings of Jesus.

As is evident from the writings of prominent liberation theologians, Marxism takes a subordinate role in defining the meaning of praxis. Marx's idea of praxis serves as means of analysis which Latin American liberation theologians have in some ways found useful and in other ways rejected in analyzing their own historical context (see chapter 7). In the Latin American context, they have favored a form of socialism as offering the most promise for a just future on their continent. In doing so, however, they have been conscientious about the ideological consequences of their own thinking, especially as they have ventured a critical appropriation of Marxism. Most importantly, they have reasoned in accordance with the resources of the Christian theological tradition.

Walter Altmann, in *Luther and Liberation: A Latin American Perspective*, has carefully articulated the resonance between the Reformation theology of Martin Luther and the commitment of liberation theology to freedom, including freedom in the economic sphere. The doctrine of justification by grace through faith in Christ alone liberates the Christian person to serve as neighbor to the least of these: "sharecroppers, small farmers, employees, the unemployed, factory workers, immigrants, refugees, people of color, native peoples, women, children."[39] According to the theology of the cross, the Christian person is sent to engage in good works that are efficacious in both unmasking the idols of this world in God's right hand kingdom and serving the cause of justice in God's left

---

38. Cf. Gutiérrez, *Theology of Liberation*, 231–32.

39. Walter Altmann, *Luther and Liberation: A Latin American Perspective*, trans. Mary M. Solberg (Minneapolis: Fortress, 1992) 145.

hand kingdom.[40] In Latin America this means engagement in the praxis of "critical-active transformation" based on the reality of two particular social conditions: "(1) the recognition of a fundamentally unjust system, characterized by social oppression; and (2) the existence of concrete possibilities of action, given by the historical process the immediate circumstances."[41]

Liberation theology's idea of praxis may indeed "serve as a challenge to all static views of truth and reality" and "help to remind theology that the biblical view of truth and revelation is inextricably linked to the ongoing transformation of reality, one that is oriented to the future (eschatology) and guided by the promise of freedom."[42] The context of liberation theology is tragically characterized by chronic hunger and the diseases of the poor. Although Luther labeled James as a "straw epistle" and would have preferred it not be included in the New Testament canon, it nevertheless remains within the canon with the insistent claim that "faith by itself, if it has no works, is dead" (Jas 2:17). Thereby the strong message of James serves as a challenge to the quietism which has too often tragically ennervated Christian social ethics. If the final judgment by the Son of Man takes place according to what has been done to serve the hungry and thirsty, the naked and imprisoned (Matt 25:31–46), then the challenge of liberation praxis requires nothing less than obedience.

---

40. Ibid., 75–80.
41. Ibid., 83.
42. Braaten, "Praxis: The Trojan Horse of Liberation Theology," 279.

6

Basic Christian Communities

The Agent of Liberation Theology

WHILE CRITICS HAVE FOCUSSED on the use of Marxism as a form of social analysis and the possibility of violent revolution as a means of social change in describing the praxis of Latin American liberation theology (see chapter 7), the primary agency for embodying liberation theology unfolded in the proliferation of basic Christian communities across the landscape in both Roman Catholic parishes and Protestant congregations. This ancient, yet innovative initiative in "being church" breathed new life into the dry bones of the institution. This chapter begins with an overview of the origins and ecclesiological orientation of the basic Christian communities movement in Latin America. It continues with a description of the symbiotic relationship between liberation theology and these communities. In a third section we examine life in the basic Christian communites, identifying four key aspects: communities of the poor, the encounter with the Bible as good news for the poor, the change in consciousness from fatalism to activism, and the prophetic and practical activity. In conclusion, this chapter looks briefly at the challenge posed by these communities for the institutional church and the impact on the renewal of the church in other contexts.

ORIGINS AND ECCLESIOLOGICAL ORIENTATION

One of the most influential catalysts for the basic Christian communities movement in Latin America was the pathbreaking work of Paulo Freire in the field of popular education. Freire launched an innovative method of literacy training among the poor that was adopted in many parts of the continent. At the end of the 1950s, Freire began this educational work at the University of Recife in northeast Brazil.[1] The aim of his literacy efforts was *conscientization*, the capacity to claim one's own dignity and voice in the face of abject social conditions and poverty. "The foundation of Freire's approach was the mutuality of respect between the teacher (as teacher-student) and student (as student-teacher). In this dialogue, the students would explore the world of oppression together as it was experienced in the everyday lives of the people."[2]

Freire's methodology was about much more than literacy training, however. It aimed at nothing less than a new political awareness and activism on the part of poor and oppressed people. Literacy meant not only the ability to read but a new capacity for agency as the determinors of their own destiny. Conventional literacy stirred political and cultural literacy. For example, the selection of materials for the literacy curriculum addressed matters of economic and political concern. As a consequence of this agenda, Freire's methods were received by the ruling classes as subversive and revolutionary. The coup in Brazil in 1964 brought repression to these efforts and Freire was exiled to Chile in the same year. Nevertheless, these educational efforts greatly influenced the pedagogy that emerged in the basic Christian communities.

Early efforts at the renewal of the church trace back as early as the 1940s and 1950s in the form of popular catechesis and weekly meetings for prayer and Bible study. The strengthening of lay leadership helped to build a sense of partnership with the ministry of clergy. In the 1960s the emergence of the basic Christian communities movement occurred as a dimension of parish revival authorized by Latin American bishops and priests in the spirit of Vatican II. *Lumen Gentium* emphasized the church's active involvement in the affairs of the world and *Gaudium et Spes* authorized diocesan efforts to deepen and broaden ecclesial participation by the people of the parishes.[3] The traditional ecclesial hierarchy opened itself to reform by taking seriously the vital involvement of the people of God in relation to the pastoral ministry of the institutional church. This meant new engagement on the part of the poor and destitute

---

1. For this and the following, David Tombs, *Latin American Liberation Theology* (Boston: Brill, 2002) 94–96.

2. Tombs, *Latin American Liberation Theology*, 94. The classic work describing Freire's approach is *Pedagogy of the Oppressed*, trans. M. Ramos (New York: Continuum, 1970).

3. Tombs, *Latin American Liberation Theology*, 171.

laity in church life in local communities, taking with new seriousness engagement in changing oppressive social conditions. Papal authorization of the basic Christian communities movement was granted with the issuing of the encyclical *Evangelii Nuntiandi: Apostolic Exhortation on Evangelization in the Modern World* by Pope Paul VI in 1975, which endorsed the importance of these communities for the renewal of the church.[4] For example, by the late 1970s the nurture of the basic Christian communities was named as one of the four central pastoral priorities by the Brazilian bishops.

The confluence of many complex ecclesial and social factors thus led to the explosion of the basic Christian communities movement. Among these were "the emerging consciousness of the dependency of Latin American countries on the First World and the need to struggle for justice and liberation; the shortage of priests, resulting in new roles for the laity and the religious sisters; Vatican II's recognition of 'human development' as part of evangelization; movements and programs that served to raise the literacy level and social consciousness of the people; the insistence of prophetic bishops on the necessary integration of Christian faith and social action; and the example of the Protestant sects' knowledge of the Bible and the vitality of their religious gatherings."[5]

The basic Christian communities movement provided the provocation for a dramatic transformation of traditional Roman Catholic ecclesial paradigm into a liberation ecclesiology. In this striking reformation of the church, new priorities and characteristics found expression. Liberation ecclesiology gave impetus to a new pattern of ecclesial existence, characterized as "the church of the poor," "the church of the poor as people of God," "church at the service of the reign of God," and "church as sacrament of historic liberation."[6] Charismatic revival in both the Roman Catholic and Protestant parishes added "the rediscovery of the Holy Spirit" as another potent force in the renewal of ecclesiology in Latin America.[7]

---

4. Ibid., 167.

5. Ana Maria Tepedino, "Basic Ecclesial Communities," in *The SCM Dictionary of Third World Theologies*, ed. Virginia Fabella and R. S. Sugirtharajah, trans. Phillip Berryman (London: SCM, 2003) 12.

6. Sergio Torrez Gonzalez, "Ecclesiologies—Latin American," in *The SCM Dictionary of Third World Theologies*, ed. Fabella and Sugirtharajah, trans. Phillip Berryman, 77.

7. Ibid., 78.

THE VITALITY OF LIBERATION THEOLOGY

LIBERATION THEOLOGY AND BASIC CHRISTIAN COMMUNITIES

The theology of liberation has found its most vital expression in the many basic Christian communities which dotted the Latin America landscape. Both liberation theology and the basic Christian communities emerged at the conclusion of the gestation period which ran from Vatican II to Medellín. Vatican II's recognition that the church of the Third World must be "a church of the poor" prepared the way for the Latin American bishops to encourage the development of basic Christian communities at their Medellín Conference.[8] References to the basic Christian communities are frequent throughout the literature of liberation theology and provide a concrete expression of the kind of living theology which liberation theology seeks to promote. Phrases such as "popular church," "church of the poor," or "poor church" are attempts to describe a church in which liberation theology is not just theory but is actually lived in communities of the poor. The symbiotic relationship between liberation theology and basic Christian communities can be observed by the way these communities have taken up many of the concerns for liberation into their praxis, grounded in a certain way of reading Scripture (see chapter 4). Likewise, liberation theology has itself been nurtured as it has incorporated the insights which arise from the biblical interpretation and engagement of the poor.

The basic Christian communities emerged from the awareness by many within the institutional church that it must develop a closer relationship with the people who constitute it. In Latin America this has meant a closer relationship with the poor. While some have come to speak of "two" churches in Latin American, distinguishing between the institutional church and the basic Christian communities, such a distinction masks the truth that the basic Christian communities have lived in an intimate relationship with the institutional church structure. Nevertheless, it is important to acknowledge the friction which also arose between the agenda of the church hierarchy and the basic Christian communities with their own vision of what the church can and ought to be. This is especially true where the leadership of the church, the bishops and

---

8. Cf. Alvaro Barreiro, *Basic Ecclesial Communities: The Evangelization of the Poor*, trans. Barbara Campbell (Maryknoll, NY: Orbis, 1982) 4–7.

hierarchy, has not shared the emphasis on liberation as it developed in the basic Christian communities.[9]

A concise and colorful description of the basic Christian communities was offered by Penny Lernoux:

> Composed of small groups of neighbors (no more than twenty adults) in impoverished rural villages and urban slums, the communities usually start as a spin-off from the parish Church by relieving the hard-pressed priest of such duties as catechism classes. In sharing the responsibilities of the Church, community members often begin to share in other neighborhood concerns, such as a health center or a school. Because religious instruction emphasizes Medellín's concern with "liberating education," the Bible is read as a story of liberation. By applying biblical stories to their own situation, community members perceive an essential parallel: if the God of the Bible was on the side of the poor and oppressed back then, God must be on their side, too. This knowledge is the beginning of the end of the colonial inheritance of fatalism. Children do not die because it is God's will; they die because of lack of food and medicine and unhygenic living conditions. In understanding reality, community members want to change their situation, through cooperatives, a shanty-town association or similar intermediate organizations that enable them to have some voice in their own destiny. In effect, the communities are practicing their own theology of liberation.[10]

Other accounts of the basic Christian communities present similar descriptions of the fundamental aspects which make up the experience of these communities. For example, Jether Pereira Ramalho included people's participation, the option for the poor, the rediscovery of the gospel, analyzing reality, and the propriety of the interests of the community over those of "the Church" as characteristics of the basic Christian communities.[11] Similarly, Raul Vidales emphasized a ministry in the basic Christian communities which is prophetic (cf. cultic), democratic (cf. hierarchical), "proletarian" (cf. elite), popular (cf. "clericalized."), cre-

---

9. For a concrete example of the kinds of tension experienced between basic Christian communities and hierarchy, see Rob Cogswell, "The Church in Cuernavaca," *Christian Century* 100 (1983) 1161–64.

10. Penny Lernoux, "The Long Path to Puebla," in *Puebla and Beyond*, ed. John Eagleson and Philip Scharper, trans. John Drury (Maryknoll, NY: Orbis, 1979) 19.

11. See Jether Pereira Ramalho, "Basic Popular Communities in Brazil: Some Notes of Pastoral Activity in Two Types," *Ecumenical Review* 29 (1977) 395–98.

ative (cf. administrative and authoritarian), and in service to the popular struggle for liberation (cf. "feudal" and paternalistic).[12] Such descriptions suggest some differences and points of tension between the basic Christian communities and the traditional experience of the church in Latin America.

LIFE IN BASIC CHRISTIAN COMMUNITIES: FOUR ASPECTS

In sorting through the manifold and diverse testimonies in the life of the basic Christian communities, four aspects deserve special emphasis. *First*, the basic Christian communities are *communities of the poor*. Most often the communities are not even led by clergy but by poor people themselves who have received guidance and direction from other communities and from clergy who support the development of the communities.

> Each community consists of a few poor Christians. When a group gains 15 or 20 members, it splits into two communities. Members continue to be active in ordinary church services, but, in addition, each community meets once a week to study the Bible, to pray and to talk about life in light of the Bible.[13]

What the members of these communities share first of all is their experience as poor persons who view life from the perspective of their socioeconomic location. It is this point of view which is fundamental to the experience of the basic Christian communities. Most of the communities (at least in Brazil) arose in rural areas, but many were also located in the slum areas of cities;[14] in these poor areas, "It has been noted that the most underprivileged have been the ones most receptive to the ecclesial notion."[15]

A *second* aspect of these communities is their *encounter with the Bible as good news for the poor*. The most well-known documentation of reading and interpreting the Bible by the poor remains that of Ernesto Cardenal's *The Gospel in Solentiname*, which provides excerpts from the conversations of the poor at Solentiname, Nicaragua, on biblical texts.

---

12. See Raul Vidales, "People's Church and Christian Ministry," *International Review of Mission* 66 (1977) 46.

13. Cogswell, "Church in Cuernavaca," 1162.

14. Barreiro, *Basic Ecclesial Communities*, 8. Cf. the specific examples of what is meant by communities of the poor, 9–13.

15. As quoted in ibid., 13.

Basic Christian Communities

A more systematic treatment of the relevance of the Bible for the basic Christian communities has been provided by Alvaro Barreiro.[16] Barreiro highlights the correspondence between biblical concern for the poor and the experience of the poor who read the Bible in the basic Christian communities. All types of literature in the Bible—Old and New Testaments, gospels and epistles, law and promise—receive an existentially relevant interpretation when read from the point of view of the poor. Barriero provides insight into the way in which the privileged position of the poor as those addressed by the biblical promises is disclosed as they read the Bible from within the context of the basic Christian communities today:

> The "message" which is addressed to us today, when we hear the proclamation of the good news of the Kingdom of God to the poor, is that we must love the poor as God loves them, with a preferential love that will liberate them concretely and historically from the unjust oppression which they are suffering. Anyone who does not strive to put an end to the suffering of the poor by becoming involved in their liberation is dissociated from and opposed to God's saving plan.[17]

Such a conclusion regarding God's partiality toward the poor is not just the personal opinion of Barriero but a conviction which arises in the hearts of the poor themselves as they read the Bible for its liberating message.

The *third* aspect of the basic Christian communities which deserves special attention is *the change in consciousness from fatalism to activism*. In encountering the Bible's good news for the poor, a radical shift in consciousness takes place among those who experience basic Christian community. They learn that God is not the cause of their poverty but rather the one who gives occasion for their hopes for liberation.

> Slowly they began to understand that their hunger, their diseases, their infant mortality, their unemployment, their unpaid wages, were not the will of God, but the result of the greed of a few Salvadorans and of their own passivisim.[18]

Having discovered that God's will for their lives is not the continuation of poverty and injustice, the poor begin to explore and analyze the causes

---

16. Cf. ibid., 14–45.

17. Ibid., 49.

18. Rutilio Grande, as quoted by Alan Riding, "Latin Church in Siege," *New York Times Magazine* (May 6, 1979) 42, regarding his experience in El Salvador.

for their condition. Fatalism gives way to conscientization about the social, economic, and political factors which contribute to their poverty. In the process of raising consciousness which takes place in the basic Christian communities, one participant names an essential element: "The good thing about this movement of ours is that we feel like real human beings."[19] This citation speaks profoundly of the "conversion experience" which takes place in the basic Christian communities.

The *fourth* and final aspect involves *the prophetic and practical activity* undertaken by the basic Christian communities to address their situation. The new consciousness, awakened by biblical study, gives rise to specific forms of engagement based on the needs of a given community. Constructing housing, developing a health center, organizing farmers against oppression, organizing workers into unions, serving as leaders in parishes, or becoming involved in the political process are examples of the activities which flow naturally out of the new consciousness born in the members of basic Christian communities.[20] In these ways the members of the communities begin to live out the faith insights they have discovered through their encounter with God in Scripture and with one another.

CHALLENGE AND INFLUENCE OF THE BASIC CHRISTIAN COMMUNITIES

It is striking how the basic Christian communities incarnate the basic elements of liberation theology. In a lived encounter with their social environment, the poor through commitment, social analysis, and theological reflection based on communal Bible study engage in concrete action to improve their lives. In the basic Christian communities the poor begin to take responsibility for their own destiny, encouraged by their faith in the God who sides with the poor.

Theologians of liberation expressed great hope in the potential of the basic Christian communities to reshape the future of Latin America. Barreiro, for example, wrote about hope for a mission of the poor in evangelizing both the rich and the church as a whole. Regarding the evangelizing of the rich, Barreiro writes:

> Therefore, when the oppressed poor accept the gospel as good news of liberation, and actually strive to become liberated from

---

19. As quoted by Barreiro, *Basic Ecclesial Communities*, 54.
20. Cf. the detailed examples offered in ibid., 52–61.

Basic Christian Communities

the oppression that is being suffered, they are, ipso facto, battling against the sin of the oppressor, inciting the latter to conversion, and are making the greatest gesture of Christian love toward the latter. It is in this paradoxical way that the poor of the [basic Christian communities] proclaim the good news of liberation to the rich who are oppressing them.[21]

The poor are called to evangelize a church which is often tempted by quantitative measures of power and success.

Gustavo Gutiérrez addresses the evangelizing potential of the poor, an evangelizing which begins with the church itself:

Evangelization will be really liberating when the poor themselves are the bearers of the gospel message. Then, to preach the gospel will be a gospel "unpresentable in society." It will be expressed in an unrefined manner, it will smell bad. The Lord, who hardly has the figure of a person (cf. the Canticles of the Servant of Yahweh in Isaiah) will speak to us in the voices of the poor. Only in listening to that voice will we recognize him as our liberator.[22]

This theme recurs throughout the writings of Gutiérrez and other liberation theologians who view the awakening of the poor taking place in basic Christian communities as the most profound development to which liberation theology has contributed.[23]

The impact of basic Christian communities on their socioeconomic and political contexts has frequently aroused significant conflict and opposition. Largely this is a consequence of the transformative praxis advocated and pursued by the members of these communities. For example, from 1964 to 1985, the members of basic Christian communities engaged in fierce struggle with the military government and elite classes in Brazil over the use of the land and the preservation of the rainforest.[24] Madeleine Cousineau Adriance draws this strong conclusion from her extensive research into this exemplary case history:

---

21. Ibid., 67.

22. Gustavo Gutiérrez, "Freedom and Salvation: A Political Problem," in *Liberation and Change*, ed. Ronald H. Stone, trans. Alvin Gutiérrez (Atlanta: John Knox, 1977) 93.

23. Cf. references to the subversive power of the poor in Gustavo Gutiérrez, *The Power of the Poor in History*, trans. Robert R. Barr (Maryknoll, NY: Orbis, 1983).

24. Madeleine Cousineau Adriance, *Promised Land: Base Christian Communities and the Struggle for the Amazon* (Albany: State University of New York Press, 1995).

The Vitality of Liberation Theology

> It should be clear from the participation of the [basic Christian communities] members in unions and in land occupations, from the degree of violence against them, and from the results of these occupations, that base communities have been having an impact on the structure of agrarian relations of production in Maranhão, Pará, and Tocantins. Thus, it may be said that they have been functioning as a prophetic movement. Another aspect of rural life that has been challenged by the [basic Christian communities] members is sexual inequality. This is important in relation to the land struggle because of the contribution to that struggle made by women who are freeing themselves from traditional gender expectations.[25]

Such active engagement typifies the praxis of basic Christian communities across Latin America in challenging unjust and inhumane working and living conditions through organized direct action campaigns. Moreover here as elsewhere, bold confrontation with the economic and political status quo provoked countless instances of opposition and repressive violence from those threatened by movements for social justice.

Liberation theologians themselves were not immune to acts of silencing and even violence, because of their participation in the reformation of the popular church through the basic Christian communities. The most notable instance of Vatican censure against a prominent liberation theologian was directed against Leonardo Boff, especially because of his criticism of the institutional church in his book *Church: Charism and Power—Liberation Theology and the Institutional Church*, published in Brazil in 1981.[26] In May 1984, Boff was summoned to Rome to give account for his challenge to the institutional church as presented in this work. In September 1984, the Sacred Congregation for the Doctrine of the Faith issued its "Instruction on Certain Aspects of Liberation Theology" to draw attention to deficiencies in the theology of liberation (see chapter 8). As a consequence of the book on ecclesiology and his examination of its contents, Boff was sentenced to eleven months of "obsequious silence" for having described the character of the institutional church, among other things, as feudal and elitist. If advocacy for the poor was one

---

25. Ibid., 139.

26. Leonardo Boff, *Church: Charism and Power—Liberation Theology and the Institutional Church*, trans. John W. Diercksmeier (London: SCM, 1985).

Basic Christian Communities

thing, criticism of the institutional church appeared to be another thing altogether.

Social and political awakening of the poor through the agency of the basic Christian communities could lead to even more severe consequences than church discipline. On November 16, 1989, six Jesuit priests, together with their housekeeper and her daughter, were murdered by military forces in El Salvador.[27] Among them was the prominent liberation theologian Ignacio Ellacuría. Another likely intended victim was the liberation theologian Jon Sobrino. These eight martyrs joined the seventy-five thousand others who had already been killed in El Salvador's brutal civil war. These deaths symbolized the cost of discipleship paid by countless other members of basic Christian communities, whose names are little known but whose courageous witness lives on in local memory.

The effect of thousands of basic Christian communities in Latin America in the last decades (eighty thousand were estimated to exist in Brazil alone in 1979) has exercised significant impact on the church and society in Latin America.

> Thus there are those who believe that the CEBs have become the single most important aspect of the evolution of a less authoritarian and more participatory society in general.[28]

Whereas the interest of liberation theologians in Marxism has received inordinate attention by outside observers and critics of liberation theology, Latin America society has been influenced much more by the message of the Bible as it has been read, interpreted, and practiced by the members of these thousands of basic Christian communities than by advocates of revolution cast in the Marxist mold. The theology of liberation through the basic Christian communities has functioned more as a means of subverting the prevailing unjust order than as a threat to sudden revolution.[29]

The phenomenon of basic Christian communities in Latin America has influenced the shape of church reform in many other settings across the globe. Margaret Hebblethwaite has advocated four translatable

27. Jon Sobrino, Ignacio Ellacuría, et al., *Companions of Jesus: The Jesuit Martyrs of El Salvador* (Maryknoll, NY: Orbis, 1990).

28. Allan Figueroa Deck, "Forward to the English Translations," in *Basic Ecclesial Communities*, ed. Barreiro, xii–xiii. This judgment is shared by Daniel H. Levine, "Religion and Politics: Dimensions of Renewal," *Thought* 59 (1984) 133–35.

29. Cf. Rubem Alves, "God's People and Man's Liberation," *Communio Viatorum* 14 (1971) 114–15.

dimensions of basic Christian communities for other contexts. "Base communities" are: (1) the basic cell of the church, (2) about the basics of Christianity, (3) about the base of society—the poor, and (4) about the base of the church—the laity.[30] Stories about the impact of basic Christian communities originate from places as diverse as the Iona Community in Scotland, the house churches of China, the home churches of Australia, the slums of the Philippines, or small towns in Spain.[31] The small group movement within congregations in the United States also has been influenced significantly by the model of basic Christian communities in Latin America.[32]

The emergence of numerous, vibrant Latin American basic Christian communities provides a mirror by which North American churches can better view themselves. Are there ways in which the North American churches need to be evangelized by the poor Christians of the Third World? Are these biblical passages about God's expectation for justice, which an affluent church relegates to the periphery of Scripture? Why are these biblical passages about God's expectation for justice relegated to the periphery of scripture by an affluent church? Is there a concrete praxis for churches in the First World to undertake in advocating and implementing policies which serve the needs of those who are poor?

Paul employed the image of the body with its many members to portray the church of Christ (1 Cor 12). If the body of Christ consists on a global scale not only of the congregational life familiar to us but also the life of the basic Christian communities, we find ourselves intricately connected to one another in ways once unimagined. The basic Christian communities of Latin America give renewed poignancy to Paul's assertion, "If one member suffers, all suffer together" (1 Cor 12:26a).

---

30. Margaret Hebblethwaite, *Base Communities: An Introduction* (London: Paulist, 1994).

31. Ian M. Fraser, *Many Cells, One Body: Stories from Small Christian Communities* (Geneva: WCC, 2003).

32. Thomas A. Kleissler, Margo A. Lebert, and Mary C. McGuinness, *Small Christian Communities: A Vision of Hope for the Twenty-First Century* (Mahwah, NJ: Paulist, 2003) 15.

7

Two Questions

Marxism and Violence?

TWO OF THE MOST prevalent and trenchant criticisms of liberation theology raised by critics have been questions about (1) the use of Marxism as an instrument of social analysis and (2) the use of violence as a means of social change. These two questions were raised in a poignant and challenging way by the Sacred Congregation for the Doctrine of the Faith in the 1984 document, "Instruction on Certain Aspects of the 'Theology of Liberation.'" The issue of the use of Marxist analysis was addressed in Section 7 with this claim:

> In the case of Marxism, in the particular sense given to it in this context, a preliminary critique is all the more necessary since the thought of Marx is such a global vision of reality that all data received from observation and analysis are brought together in a philosophical and ideological structure, which predetermines the significance and importance attached to them ...
>
> Thus no separation of the parts of this epistemologically unique complex is possible. If one tries to take only one part, say, the analysis, one ends up having to accept the entire ideology.[1]

In a parallel way a sharp critique is raised about the advocacy of violence by liberation theologians, based on Marxism, as a means of social change:

> The fundamental law of history, which is the law of the class struggle, implies that society is founded on violence. To the violence which constitutes the relationship of domination of the rich over

---

1. Sacred Congregation for the Doctrine of the Faith, "Instruction on Certain Aspects of the 'Theology of Liberation'" (Vatican City: Vatican Polyglott, 1984) 17–18.

the poor, there corresponds the counter-violence of the revolution, by means of which this domination will be reversed.²

Both with regard to the use of Marxism and the possible option for violence as a means of social change, the Sacred Congregation for the Doctrine of the Faith under Cardinal Joseph Ratzinger issued a strong warning.

On the basis of such suspicions about liberation theology, particular liberation theologians have been singled out for doctrinal examination and church discipline. For example, Leonardo Boff was silenced by the Vatican in 1985.³ "The Instruction on Certain Aspects of the 'Theology of Liberation'" became a major source for issuing such judgements. Subsequently, other liberation theologians also faced examination and the threat of discipline, including Gustavo Gutiérrez and Jon Sobrino.

Two of the strongest criticisms against Latin American liberation theology posed by North American critics have been exactly its use of Marxism and its advocacy of violence.⁴ This chapter examines the discussion of Marxism as an instrument of social analysis and the appeal to violence as a means of social change to clarify the actual state of these questions in liberation thought. We will leave it to a subsequent chapter to evaluate these arguments and to the reader to decide the validity of the claims of critics regarding these two questions. A more probing analysis would further investigate the anthropology implicit in Marxist thought and the question of the reality of sin.⁵

MARXISM AS AN INSTRUMENT OF SOCIAL ANALYSIS

"[Liberation] theologians did not set out to become Marxists."⁶ It was rather the nature of Latin American reality which led liberation theologians to recognition of the need for social analysis. It was the need for an appropriate form of social analysis that prompted "not a few Latin American theologians and ministers to be so uninhibitedly open to Marxist

---

2. Ibid., 21.

3. Harvey Cox, *The Silencing of Leonardo Boff: The Vatican and the Future of World Christianity* (Oak Park, IL: Meyer-Stone, 1988).

4. Craig L. Nessan, *Orthopraxis or Heresy: The North American Theological Response to Latin American Liberation Theology* (Atlanta: Scholars, 1989) 223–38.

5. Cf. ibid., 356–58.

6. Phillip E. Berryman, "Latin American Liberation Theology," *Theological Studies* 34 (1973) 374.

categories, analyses, and interpretations of historical processes."[7] While liberation theologians have been essentially "open to Marxist categories," that does not mean they have been uncritical or doctrinaire in their use of Marxist analysis. This section will draw from the diverse references to Marxism made by liberation theologians, references which reflect the diversity of Marxism itself, in order to demonstrate the way liberation theology has employed Marxism as an instrument of social analysis.[8]

A helpful starting point for understanding the use of Marxism by the theology of liberation is the central thesis offered by José Míguez Bonino in his book *Christians and Marxists: The Mutual Challenge to Revolution*, an extensive study of the relationship between Christianity and Marxism:

> It is my thesis that, as Christians, confronted by the inhuman conditions of existence prevailing in the continent, they have tried to make their Christian faith historically relevant, they have been increasingly compelled to seek an analysis and historical program for their Christian obedience. At this point, the dynamics of the historical process both in its objective conditions and its theoretical development have led them, through the failure of several remedial and reformist alternatives to discover the unsubstitutable relevance of Marxism.[9]

Before describing the ways in which liberation theologians employ Marxism as a form of social analysis, one must clarify what is meant by the term "Marxism." Arthur F. McGovern distinguishes helpfully between the terms "Communism," "Socialism," and "Marxism."[10] "Communism" refers to those "actual political-economic systems in countries which claim to have embodied Marxist ideas" (for example, the Communist Party of the Soviet Union, China, or any other official Communist Party). "Socialism" refers to "any actual or proposed economic system which ad-

---

7. Aharon Sapezian, "Ministry with the Poor: An Introduction," *International Review of Mission* (Jan 1977) 9.

8. Robert McAfee Brown, "A Preface and a Conclusion," in *Theology in the Americas*, ed. Sergio Torres and John Eagleson (Maryknoll, NY: Orbis, 1976) xvii–xviii, warns about how the "Marxist" label is often employed in the United States to discredit an opposing position. Brown exposes this tactic and encourages evaluating liberation theology by its truth claims, rather than dismissing it prejudicially.

9. José Míguez Bonino, *Christians and Marxists: The Mutual Challenge to Revolution* (London: Hodder & Stoughton, 1976) 19.

10. See Arthur F. McGovern, *Marxism: An American Christian Perspective* (Maryknoll, NY: Orbis, 1980) 3.

vocates 'public ownership of property.'" "Marxism," by contrast, refers "to the theory or body of ideas originated by Marx and developed by others." While it is impossible to fully separate these three terms, this distinction offers a first level of clarification for what is meant by the term "Marxist," that is, the tradition founded by the writings of Karl Marx.

A second level of clarification is offered by Gregory Baum, who distinguishes between three uses of the word Marxism: "Marxism can be understood (1) as a philosophy, (2) as a plan of political action, and (3) as an instrument of social analysis."[11] The theologians of liberation by and large reject the first understanding of Marxism as a philosophy, while taking up and incorporating the second and third meanings. Marxism as "an instrument of social analysis" is the focus of discussion in this section. The role of Marxism "as a plan of political action" for changing Latin American social structures will be taken up in the next section of this chapter.

When Christians are faced with Marxism, Clodovis Boff argues that they can react in one of two ways.[12] Confronted by those aspects of Marxism which are irreconcilable with Christian faith, they can either totally reject Marxism (including its use as a theoretical and practical tool) or they can approach Marxism critically (employing those aspects of Marxist thought which are useful for social analysis while rejecting those aspects which are contradictory to Christian faith). Clearly, the second option has been taken by liberation theologians. Before describing those aspects of Marxism which have been positively appropriated by liberation theology for the purpose of social analysis, it is important to recognize those aspects of Marxism which are criticized or rejected. Here follows a brief typology of the use of Marxism by liberation theology. Six negative criticisms of Marxism by liberation theologians are followed by six positive affirmations of Marxism as an instrument for social analysis.

The *first* and most serious negative criticism of Marxism is that *it cannot be accepted as a comprehensive worldview*. Clodovis Boff distinguishes between Marxism as "historical materialism" and Marxism as "dialectical materialism."[13] By historical materialism is meant Marxism in its function as a method for analyzing society and history. This can be

11. Gregory Baum, "The Christian Left at Detroit," in *Theology in the Americas*, ed. Torres and Eagleson, 423.

12. Cf. Clodovis Boff, *Theologie und Praxis*, 113.

13. Ibid., 110.

affirmed. What cannot be accepted, however, is Marxism as "dialectical materialism." As dialectical materialism Marxism elevates itself to an all-inclusive worldview claiming ultimate validity as an explanation for all of human existence. Míguez Bonino explains how such claims by Marxism transcend its legitimate function as a form of social analysis and thereby contradict Christian faith as the only legitimate Christian worldview: "... it presents itself as a total, all-embracing, self-sufficient and exclusive understanding of reality; as exhaustive and absolute and therefore ruling out all reality and relationships outside its purview. In so doing it flatly contradicts the Christian faith and raises for itself problems which seem to me unsolvable, as the very history of Marxism indicates."[14] Insofar as Marxism exalts itself into an all-encompassing worldview, it has been rejected by liberation theologians.

The *second* negative criticism is that *the atheism of Marxism must be rejected*. This does not mean that the liberation theologians do not make use of Marx's critique of religion. Rather, Marx's critique of the ideological manipulation of religion has been employed extensively to unmask the many idols which vie for divinity in the Latin American context.[15] Nevertheless, liberation theologians go beyond Marxism's rejection of religion (which issues in atheism) and affirm the God who is truly God.

> Marx is not heterodox because he is an atheist (in regard to the idol, to money). He is heterodox because he is not enough of an atheist, because in his failure to affirm the "God-other" he is left with a system that has no outside support and no radical critique. Christianity is atheistic in regard to every idol—this it shares with Marx; but it is more critical than Marx because, in affirming the "God-other," it is critical of every *possible* system and will be until the eschatological times, until the end.[16]

A major task facing liberation theologians is that in "going against the views of dogmatic Marxists, those involved must spell out a *theory of religion* advocating *liberation*."[17] The atheism of Marx must be rejected in

14. Míguez Bonino, *Christians and Marxists*, 97.

15. Cf. Franz Hinkelammert, "The Economic Roots of Idolatry: Entrepreneurial Metaphysics," in Pablo Richard, et al., *The Idols of Death and the God of Life: A Theology*, trans. Barbara E. Campbell and Bonnie Shepard (Maryknoll, NY: Orbis, 1983) 165–93.

16. Enrique Dussel, *Ethics and the Theology of Liberation*, trans. Bernard F. McWilliams (Maryknoll, NY: Orbis, 1978) 17.

17. Dussel, "Current Events in Latin America," in *The Challenge of Basic Christian Communities*, ed. Torres and Eagleson, 100.

favor of a religion which affirms God as liberator, the God who is revealed in the Bible.

The *third* negative criticism of Marxism involves a *critique of its mechanistic understanding of historical change*.[18] This criticism grows out of an apparent contradiction in Marx's thought between a mechanistic understanding of historical change which takes place inevitably as a result of the given contradictions of the capitalist system and an understanding which asserts the catalytic role of human involvement in accomplishing historical change. Liberation theology is committed to the need for human participation in the liberation process. "History will not in any fatal or mechanistic way decide for men; the decision will always be a human decision."[19] Thus all mechanistic understandings of historical change are understood as counterproductive to the liberation struggle.

The *fourth* negative criticism is *a critique of the present historical systems which claim to embody Marxist thought*, such as in China and, above all, the Soviet Union.[20] Particularly reprehensible is the form of communism which prevailed in the Soviet Union under Joseph Stalin. The price paid for economic "progress" under communist regimes has been enormously high:

> We must also record the human cost of these achievements: the liquidation of certain social groups, the restrictions to liberty (while we must remember that "liberal freedoms" have little reality for economically, intellectually and even biologically submerged masses), the arbitrary exercise of power, the disruption of religious and family traditions which often give meaning and hope to the life of "the little in the land."[21]

Moreover, the loss of an ongoing critique of revolution and the dominance of self-interest are recognized as signs of "the deterioration of the historical Marxist movement in terms of its revolutionary potential."[22] While unwilling to surrender the need for socialism as an historical project, the present historical forms are judged deficient and in need of serious renewal.

18. Cf. Míguez Bonino, *Toward a Christian Political Ethics*, 40–42, and *Christians and Marxists*, 99.
19. Míguez Bonino, *Toward a Christian Political Ethics*, 41
20. Cf. Míguez Bonino, *Christians and Marxists*, 80–81, 87–91.
21. Ibid., 88.
22. Ibid., 89.

> ... as a whole, Western Marxist countries and parties are rapidly losing their credibility in the Third World and their flags are taken up by movements which are ready to revise theory and practice in terms of an effective revolutionary change and the construction of a genuine socialism.[23]

When the theologians of liberation speak of socialism, it is in terms adapted to the Latin American context, to be sharply distinguished from the established historical societies.

The *fifth* negative criticism involves a *rejection of the tendency of Marxism to a materialistic reductionism*. While Marxist thought has contributed an analysis of the economic forces which dominate modern life, and while an analysis of such economic forces in Latin America is vital, the theology of liberation entertains a broader definition of what is meant by liberation. Clearly, economic liberation is indispensable for the future of Latin America. But the vision of liberation theology transcends economic, social, and political liberation. Liberation also entails the cultural and spiritual development of human beings: liberation for full human personhood and liberation for deeper human community.[24]

The *sixth* negative criticism is *a rejection of the tendency of Marxism toward authoritarian rule*. The historical instances of Marxism, which represent dictatorial or narrowly oligarchical rule, stand in contradiction to liberation theology's affirmation of the human rights of the Latin American people. In the historical appropriation of Marxism, especially as interpreted by Lenin, the argument was made for a vanguard or elite to carry out the leadership in the period of transition from capitalism to the final "dictatorship of the proletariat." In those systems, however, the role of the vanguard or elite has tended to degenerate into an inflexible, authoritarian, dictatorial rule. Segundo has been at the forefront of those grappling with this problem.[25] While there remain many unresolved issues regarding their use of Marxism, liberation theologians affirm the right of the people of Latin America to a form of liberation that precludes authoritarian rule.

---

23. Ibid., 91.

24. Cf. Gutiérrez, *Theology of Liberation*, 36–37. Such a vision may not so much oppose Marx as it does the historical systems which have claimed the name of Marxist.

25. Cf. Segundo, "Mass Man-Minority Elite-Gospel Message," in *Liberation of Theology*, 208–40.

These six negative criticisms of Marxism help clarify the critical appropriation of Marxist thought by liberation theologians. Having summarized these six negative criticisms, the following six positive affirmations have been made for Marxism as an instrument of social analysis.

The *first* affirmation is a general one, *a recognition of the ethical humanism of Marx*. Especially the writings of the early Marx are filled with passionate concern for social and economic justice.[26] "The burning fire of moral indignation at man's inhumanity to man smolders below the surface of even the most abstruse theoretical analyses of the early Marxists."[27] This sense of moral indignation corresponds to the experience of liberation theologians as they encounter Latin American reality. Moreover, they realize a deep affinity between the prophetic humanism of Marx and the biblical demand for justice.[28]

The *second* positive affirmation involves *the necessity of ideological suspicion for social analysis*. Marx, Freud, and Nietzsche have been described as "masters of suspicion." Suspicion about the prevailing ideology on the part of liberation theologians has been directed at the entire ideological superstructure of Latin America including its economic, political, social, cultural, and religious dimensions. Even more, the theologians of liberation exercise pointed suspicion against many conventional theological and exegetical formulations. One source for this ideological suspicion derives from the thought of Marx.

The *third* positive affirmation is *the need for a Marxist critique of religion*. Marx sharply criticized the use of religion for the ideological justification of political power.[29] By using religion to buttress political power, mystification takes place regarding the decisive factor, that is, support for the economic status quo. Thereby religion can rightly be called the "opiate of the people," in which "religion invests the present misery with a sacred character."[30]

Liberation theology has affirmed the constructive function of Marx's critique of religion: "The criticism of religion is valuable insofar as it is a

---

26. Cf. José Porfiro Miranda, *Marx against the Marxists: The Christian Humanism of Karl Marx*, trans. John Drury (Maryknoll, NY: Orbis, 1980) 106–35.

27. Míguez Bonino, *Christians and Marxists*, 76.

28. Cf. José Porfiro Miranda, *Marx and the Bible: A Critique of the Philosophy of Oppression*, trans. John Eagleson (Maryknoll, NY: Orbis, 1974) 293–96.

29. Cf. Míguez Bonino, *Christians and Marxists*, 42–51.

30. Ibid., 49.

criticism of bourgeois society which unveils its dynamics and provides the revolutionary proletariat with adequate theoretical instruments for carrying out its historical mission of destroying and overcoming this society."[31] Special application of Marx's critique of religion in Latin America has been directed at the traditional support offered by the Roman Catholic Church to the colonial, neo-colonial, and military forms of domination which characterize Latin American history. Likewise, the most "otherworldly" aspects of Protestantism as well as many forms of popular religion have tended to ignore or obfuscate historical explanations and have been subjected to Marxist critique. However, the Marxist critique of religion exceeds its legitimate function when it rejects religion altogether and insists upon atheism.[32]

The *fourth* positive affirmation asserts that *the idea of class struggle is an accurate description of Latin American reality.*

> The class struggle is a part of our economic, social, political, cultural, and religious reality. Its evolution, its exact extent, nuances, and variations are the object of analysis of the social sciences and pertain to the field of scientific rationality.
>
> It is undeniable that the class struggle poses problems to the universality of Christian love and the unity of the Church. But any consideration of this subject must start from two elemental points: the class struggle is a fact and neutrality in this matter is impossible.[33]

Following Marx, class struggle is recognized as a given fact.[34] Capitalist society, characterized by the concentration of economic power in the hands of those who possess the means of production, leads to an increasing division between rich and poor. This analysis of class struggle is not accepted by liberation theologians because it is Marxist, but because it adequately explains Latin American reality. When the world is viewed "from below," it appears that something like class struggle is at work. Moreover, neutrality by Christians in the face of the reality of class

---

31. Ibid., 50.

32. James F. Conway, *Marx and Jesus: Liberation Theology in Latin America* (New York: Carlton, 1973) 189–94, argued that liberation theology itself is evidence for the possibility of religion acting not only as an "opiate" but also as a force for social change.

33. Gutiérrez, *Theology of Liberation*, 273. Cf. Gustavo Gutiérrez, "Faith as Freedom: Solidarity with the Alienated and Confidence in the Future," *Horizons* 2 (1975) 33.

34. Cf. Míguez Bonino, *Christians and Marxists*, 92–93.

struggle is called into question. Liberation theologians ascertain in the Bible a God who shows partiality to the poor. Therefore, in spite of the tension which this affirmation creates for the church, the reality of class struggle cannot be set aside. The final unity sought by the church can be achieved only through a conflict-laden process of overcoming the present historical divide between those who have and those who do not.[35]

The *fifth* positive affirmation involves *the basic validity of Marx's analysis of capitalism's structure of oppression.* Prominent in this discussion has been the contribution of the economist and theologian José Porfiro Miranda.[36] The basic features of Marxist analysis begin with recognition of private ownership of the means of production. In a system of private ownership, made possible by the invention of money as a means of exchange, non-owners must sell their labor to the owners in return for payment. This is the essence of the wage system. Workers subsequently exchange their wages for those items which they require to satisfy their material needs. The wage system, however, can only be legitimate when it is based on an agreement between free and equal parties. With capitalism this presupposition is not given. Coercion is exercised both by the ideology of the capitalist system and, ultimately, by the "hidden persuader" of hunger which compels participation in the system. Moreover, a rule of law is constructed to legalize this set of relationships.

The exploitative nature of capitalism becomes more fully exposed by the mechanism of "surplus value." Because capitalism is based upon ever increasing expansion, and because capitalism upholds the legitimacy of owners to earn a profit on their investment, surplus value becomes the means by which capital is "multiplied" for the accomplishment of both expansion and profit. Surplus value is the difference between the actual worth of a worker's labor in terms of what is produced and the amount which a worker is actually paid for that labor. The goal of owners becomes the maximization of surplus value and, consequently, profit. This leads to increasing alienation between owners and workers, demonstrated by a vastly unequal distribution of wealth. Furthermore, workers in industrial capitalism are distanced from the creative outcomes of their labor, leading to a further sense of alienation. This analysis of the structure of capitalism

35. Gutiérrez, *Theology of Liberation*, 277–79.
36. Cf. José Porfiro Miranda, "Private Ownership under Challenge," in *Marx and the Bible*, 1–33, and "Revolution and Existentialism," in *Being and the Messiah: The Message of St. John*, trans. John Eagleson (Maryknoll, NY: Orbis, 1977) 1–14.

thus is claimed to reveal its ultimate logic as the pursuit of profit and the advancement of self-interest. Given the fundamental inequality between the actors in this system, capitalism results in the oppression of the "weaker" participants.

Though Miranda is among the most outspoken liberation theologians in articulating a Marxist analysis of capitalism, this analysis is implicit in liberation theology's critique of the oppressive nature of capitalism. The specific characteristics of the Latin American context (for example, the role of multinational corporations) call for particular modifications of Marxist analysis.

The *sixth* and last positive affirmation is *Marx's insistence on praxis as the final criterion of theory*. Theory (or social analysis) does not constitute the final measure of truth. Instead, "theory has meaning only as it leads to a course of action which proves significant and that action itself becomes the test of theory."[37] Hereby, liberation theologians advocate a constant interchange between theory and action, culminating with active participation in the liberation process.

This concise exposition of six negative criticisms and six positive affirmations demonstrates in summary form liberation theology's critical use of Marxism as an instrument of social analysis. Those aspects of Marxism have been stressed which liberation theologians affirm as leading to a deeper understanding of Latin American reality. For the sake of systematic presentation, these aspects of Marxism have been distinguished from the historical application of Marxism in addressing concrete political options. This distinction remains formal, however, since "the choice of analytical instrument itself implies an ethical and political stance."[38] This distinction is nonetheless useful in clarifying the complex interaction between liberation theology and Marxist thought.[39]

Having provided this critical examination of the complex relationship between Marxism and liberation theology, it is essential also to acknowledge the contribution of dependency theory to the economic analysis of Latin American poverty. Dependency theory, as articulated by Andre Gunder Frank and given critical development by John Galtung,

---

37. Míguez Bonino, *Christians and Marxists*, 93.

38. Assmann, *Theology for a Nomad Church*, 38–39.

39. Cf. John Milbank, *Theology and Social Theory: Beyond Secular Reason* (Oxford: Blackwell, 1993) 177–205, for an assessment of Marxism's critique of the logic of capitalism and the limits of Marxism's account of history and anthropology.

was endorsed by prominent liberation theologians apart from reference to Marx.[40]

> Although critics of liberation theology ascribe the dependency theory to Marxist ideology, the theory of dependence is different in its orientation from Marxist or Communist. It is certain that some socio-critical elements of Marxist thought (such as historical materialist analysis of the capitalist mode of production, ideology critique, praxis-orientation, and class struggle, among others) may be positively accepted as an instrument of social analysis. For Gutiérrez, class struggle is a given fact, a part of economic, social, political, cultural, and religious reality.[41]

Dependency theory analyzes the relationship between centers of economic power and peripheries of economic dependence both within particular countries and on a global scale. Within Latin American countries, there are centers of economic power upon which the peripheries are dependent. But even the centers of economic power in Latin American countries finally demonstrate dependency on the centers of economic power in North America and Europe on the global scale. This set of dependency relationships defines the global economic system and is a form of economic analysis that transcends Marxist thought.

Whereas dependency theory was discounted in the wake of the discrediting of communism at the disintegration of the Soviet empire, reappropriation of dependency theory could make a significant contribution to the revitalization of liberation theology. A renewed iteration of dependency theory configures dependency relationships much more complexly as a kind of global "archipelago" of centers of economic power and peripheries of economic dependency. Dependency is particularly characterized by the exploitation of cheap labor.[42] According to depen-

---

40. Andre Gunder Frank, *Latin America: Underdevelopment or Revolution: Essays on the Development of Underdevelopment and the Immediate Enemy* (New York: Monthly Review Press, 1969), and Johan Galtung, "A Structural Theory of Imperialism," *African Review* 1 (1972) 93–138. Cf. the reference to dependency theory by Gutiérrez, *A Theology of Liberation*, 84–88.

41. Paul S. Chung, "God's Mission and Emancipation: A Lutheran Theology of Justification and Economic Justice," in Paul S. Chung, Ulrich Duchrow, and Craig L. Nessan, *Liberating Lutheran Theology: Freedom for Justice and Solidarity with Others in a Global Context* (Minneapolis: Fortress, 2011) 80.

42. Ulrich Duchrow and Franz J. Hinkelammert, *Property for People, Not for Profit: Alternatives to the Global Tyranny of Capital*, trans. Elaine Griffiths et al. (New York: Zed, 2004) 146.

dency theorists, there remains an indispensable role for state intervention in the global economy, "so that the loser in the competition is not condemned to death."[43] These state interventions need to focus on two primary areas: (1) governing the production of uncompetitive simple goods and (2) prevention of non-productive capital property.[44] The application of dependency theory by liberation theologians moves economic analysis beyond Marxist categories.

THE USE OF VIOLENCE AS A MEANS OF SOCIAL CHANGE?[45]

The question about the use of violence by Christians to achieve sociopolitical change emerged in the international theological discussion in the 1960s. A significant impetus was given at the World Conference on Church and Society held in Geneva in 1966, particularly by the address, "The Revolutionary Challenge to Church and Theology," by Richard Shaull.[46] Although North American, Shaull based his address on personal experiences in Latin America and the views he presented have come to be associated with Latin American liberation theology. Liberation theologians such as Gutiérrez, however, found it necessary to distance their own position from the "theology of revolution" advocated by Shaull.

> In 1966 another line of theological reflection emerged, again with strong biblical overtones. It was known as the theology of revolution. It included, as a segment, a theology of violence, and this was the tree that often hid the forest. The theology of revolution had been developed initially by theologians who were very familiar with certain countries then engaged in a process of revolution. But it was eventually removed from its context and found a sounding board in certain currents of thought in Germany. In this latter form it was reintroduced into Latin America.[47]

---

43. Ibid., 152.

44. Cf. ibid., 152

45. Cf. McGovern, *Marxism*, 285–92, and Alfredo Fierro, *The Militant Gospel: A Critical Introduction to Political Theologies*, trans. John Drury (Maryknoll, NY: Orbis, 1977) 201–7.

46. Cf. the accounts of this conference by J. M. Lochman, "Ecumenical Theology of Revolution," *Scottish Journal of Theology* 21 (1968) 170–86, and "Peace and Revolution," *Reformed and Presbyterian World* 30 (1968) 108–14.

47. Gutiérrez, *Power of the Poor in History*, 43.

Gutiérrez is critical of the theology of revolution for several reasons. Although it served as a challenge for theology to recognize how it is implicated by unjust social orders, it went too far when it claimed that "the gospel is not only not at odds with revolution but actually calls for revolution."[48] Such "baptizing" of revolution, however, could easily be accused of succumbing to an uncritical ideology based on the misuse of biblical texts. Even more objectionable was the way the theology of revolution came to be carried out by academic theologians who applied it theoretically to revolutionary contexts. By contrast, Gutiérrez argues that the only legitimate context for such reflection must come "from within the liberation process" itself.[49]

Others, such as Monika Hellwig, have observed this process from a distance and have come to similar conclusions:

> My own incomplete survey of positions suggests that those more distant from the Latin American scene are willing to condone more violence than those actually engaged in it, perhaps because they feel it ill becomes them to prescribe for others in a far more difficult situation than they face themselves . . . Almeri Bezerra de Melo, points out that there is almost no published Latin American discussion on the question of violence from a theological perspective, and very little from either Africa or Asia, while there is a flood of literature from Europeans and North Americans interested in Latin America.[50]

Regardless of who first initiated and gave impetus to the discussion of violence, the Latin Americans soon found themselves in the midst of a debate which stimulated their own reflection on the use of violence as a means of social change.[51]

Within Latin America a "classical" statement of the issue of violence has come to expression among liberation theologians.[52] A central figure articulating this position was Dom Helder Camara.[53] Describing the

---

48. Ibid.

49. Ibid., 44.

50. Monika Hellwig, "Response of Monika Hellwig to Avery Dulles," in *Theology in the Americas*, ed. Torres and Eagleson, 103–4.

51. Cf. the viewpoints assembled in *Christianity & Crisis* 32 (1972) 163–72, especially the contribution by José Míguez Bonino, "Violence and Liberation," 169–72.

52. For a concise statement, see Berryman, "Latin American Liberation Theology," 367.

53. Cf. Dom Helder Camara, "Violence in the Modern World," in *Between Honesty*

Latin American situation of injustice as one of "institutional violence," Helder Camara articulated a viewpoint that attained authoritative status at the Medellín Conference and came to exercise considerable influence in shaping the violence problematic among liberation theologians.[54] This position begins with the recognition that revolutionary violence is not itself the only or first form of violence which needs to be examined in the Latin American context. Rather, there are three kinds of violence.

The first violence is the *institutionalized violence* which prevails in Latin America. This first violence, "practiced routinely by the power structures, is usually perfectly legal; it takes place in the haciendas and factories, banks and government ministries, the White House or Pentagon ... It is what gives the upper 5% control over half the wealth, and the lower 35% of the people 5% of the wealth."[55]

> The first and most inhuman violence that exists is that which destroys millions of people, whole generations: the violence of the oppressors, of the dominators, of the empires which are objectified in the unjust and oppressive structures that do not allow a human being to be human. And, what is worse, it makes the oppressed, because of their desperation, into oppressors themselves, as is seen in the foreman over the worker, the police over the people, and the middle class over the lower classes.[56]

The reality of violence institutionalized into Latin American structures became the fundamental starting point for the reflections of liberation theologians on violence.[57]

---

and Hope: Documents from and about the Church in Latin America, issued by the Peruvian Bishops' Commission for Social Action, trans. John Drury (Maryknoll, NY: Maryknoll Publications, 1970) 47–54.

54. Medellín Documents: "Peace" (Nos. 15–19), in *The Gospel of Peace and Justice: Catholic Social Teaching since Pope John*, ed. Joseph Gremillion (Maryknoll, NY: Orbis, 1976) 459–61.

55. Berryman, "Latin American Liberation Theology," 367.

56. Dussel, *History of the Church in Latin America* (Grand Rapids: Eerdmans, 1981) 174.

57. Cf. Segundo Galilea, "Liberation Theology and New Tasks," in *Frontiers of Theology in Latin America*, ed. Rosino Gibellini, trans. John Drury (Maryknoll, NY: Orbis, 1979) 174–77; Míguez Bonino, "Violence and Liberation," in ibid., 169–70; and Rubem Alves, "Towards a Theology of Liberation" (PhD diss., Princeton Theological Seminary, 1969) 193–98.

In response to institutionalized violence arises a second violence, namely, *counter-violence* or *revolutionary violence*. This is the violence "practiced in order to take power and establish a just order."[58] It is the violence which motivated Camilo Torres or Nestor Paz to come to the conclusion that only violence could achieve the change required in Latin America.

> Reacting to this oppressive violence is the violence of a small number who courageously challenge egoistic conformity, risk their own well-being and even their lives in order to transform the oppressor-oppressed dialectic into a relationship of brother-with-brother.[59]

Liberation theologians have claimed counter-violence as a second form of violence in their theological viewpoint. It finds a variety of applications, ranging from those who tend to use it as a justification of revolutionary violence[60] to those who are more conscientious about the ambiguity of all violence.[61]

Responding to the threat of counter-violence, there emerges what can be called a third violence, that is, *repressive violence*. It is that form of violence employed by a threatened system to suppress those who have taken up revolutionary violence. This includes those repressive measures which might be enacted by a Latin American government in order to preserve "national security." Thereby, basic human rights are violated and all dissent becomes criminal. This form of violence became intense in Latin America during the 1970s and has had a significant impact on liberation theology.

Beginning with this understanding of the distinct forms of violence, individual liberation theologians arrive at diverse conclusions regarding the use of violence as a means of social change.[62] Segundo, for example, sought to broaden the definition of violence to acknowledge that human existence cannot be lived without a certain measure of violence.[63]

---

58. Berryman, "Latin American Liberation Theology," 367.

59. Dussel, *History of the Church in Latin America*, 174–75.

60. Cf. Alves, "Towards a Theology of Liberation," 218–22.

61. Cf. Míguez Bonino, "Violence and Liberation," in *Frontiers of Theology in Latin America*, ed. Gibellini, 170–72.

62. McGovern, *Marxism*, 193.

63. Cf. Juan Luis Segundo, *Our Idea of God*, trans. John Drury (Maryknoll, NY: Orbis, 1974) 163–69, and Segundo, *Liberation of Theology*, 156–65.

The limits of human energy mean that some persons are always treated more as things than with the full respect due to human beings. This he describes as an inevitable form of violence. Moreover, Jesus can be seen as exercising violence in the sharp words he directs at the Pharisees and scribes. Segundo concludes that life must be appraised according to its inherent violence. The gospel shows how it is possible in an evolutionary historical process to learn to overcome the given reality of violence. According to Segundo, the gospel ". . . is meant to orient us in the right direction through the course of history, so that we will look for ways to replace violence with love insofar as new possibilities open up to us."[64]

Segundo brings his understanding of history as process to his treatment of the question of violence. Ignacio Ellacuría also gives considerable attention to the question of violence.[65] Like Segundo, Ellacuría broadens the definition of violence to include biological and psychoanalytical viewpoints which witness to the basic aggressiveness of human behavior. In its most extreme form, however, violence reveals a context of injustice. A Christian response to the violence caused by injustice must have its goal as "the redemption of violence." Ellacuría offers three historical examples of those who have come to strikingly different conclusions about how that redemption must take place: Charles de Foucauld, Martin Luther King Jr., and Camilo Torres. Ellacuría comes to the following conclusion:

> The eradication of violence in all its forms is an urgent task that cannot be postponed. But stress must be placed on that form of violence which is protected by legal forms, which entails the permanent establishment of an unjust disorder, which precludes the conditions required for the human growth of the person, and which therefore gives rise to strong reactions. Our rejection of violence must be absolute. The paradox is that the absolute character of this rejection calls for attitudes and lines of action that cannot help but be extreme.[66]

The ambiguous yet possible use of violence as a means of social change is perhaps nowhere better expressed.

Míguez Bonino shares this sense of the ambiguity of violence, but goes on to recognize the ambiguity of nonviolence as well: "Seen in this

64. Segundo, *Our Idea of God*, 169.

65. Ignacio Ellacuría, *Freedom Made Flesh: The Mission of Christ and His Church*, trans. John Drury (Maryknoll, NY: Orbis, 1976) 167–231.

66. Ibid., 230.

perspective, the often-debated question of nonviolence takes on a different aspect. It ceases to be a question of 'personal purity.' Strictly speaking, we do not deal with nonviolence but with qualities, forms, and limitations of violence present in a conflict of oppression and liberation."[67] Míguez Bonino seeks to move beyond the absolutizing of any single position which fails to consider the concrete situation.

When one surveys the conclusions drawn by liberation theologians regarding the use of violence as a means of social change, they range from Galilea's call for a "theology of reconciliation" as the only Christian solution[68] to Dussel's blunt opinion that he does "not believe that nonviolence is a viable option for Latin Americans who want to effect change."[69] It is somewhat surprising, given the paradigmatic significance of Helder Camara's viewpoint, that his conclusions regarding the option for nonviolence have not received more serious consideration. Similarly, the possibility of strategic nonviolence as a means of attaining social change (as it has been practiced by the 1980 winner of the Nobel Peace Prize, Adolfo Pérez Esquivel) is noticeably absent from their reflections.[70] In Argentina, Peru, Ecuador, Paraguay, and throughout Latin America, Pérez Esquivel has provided a nonviolent model for social change which should receive further consideration for the liberation struggle. Likewise, the witness of Mahatma Gandhi and Martin Luther King Jr. would seem to deserve more thorough examination.

The question about the use of violence as a means of social change, especially insofar as it conforms to Marxist theory, collides forcefully with the Christian tradition. Liberation theology has provided an insightful analysis of institutionalized, counter, and repressive violence. Liberation theologians have continued to struggle with the question of violence in the Latin American context.[71]

---

67. Míguez Bonino, "Violence and Liberation," in Frontiers of Theology in Latin America, ed. Gibellini, 172. Cf. also *Marxists and Christians*, 124.

68. Galilea, "Liberation Theology and New Tasks," in *Frontiers of Theology in Latin America*, ed. Gibellini, 176–77.

69. Dussel, *History of the Church in Latin America*, 173.

70. Cf. Adolfo Pérez Esquivel, *Christ in a Poncho: Testimonials of the Nonviolent Struggles in Latin America*, ed. Charles Antoine, trans. Robert R. Barr (Maryknoll, NY: Orbis, 1983).

71. Cf. the exchange between Dan R. Ebener, "Is There a Future for Nonviolence in Central America?" and Mano Barreno, "A Latin American Response," *Fellowship* 49 (1983) 6–7, 28.

Two Questions

This chapter has examined the provocative questions which the appeal to Marxist social analysis and the use of violence have raised against the validity of liberation theology. All attempts to simply equate liberation theology with Marxism or the advocacy of violence, however, must be viewed as gross oversimplifications. The application to Marxist social analysis and the possible use of violence as a means of social change nevertheless remain open and troubling questions.

8

Dynamics of Polarization

North American Critics versus Liberation Theology

NO THEOLOGICAL MOVEMENT HAS in recent years evoked such strong reactions as liberation theology. Not since the debate over "death of God" theology have positions among theologians and within the church been so severely polarized. A survey of the North American literature in response to Latin American liberation theology reveals sharply divided opinion about the merits and liabilities of liberation theology.[1] This chapter examines several major factors contributing to the controversy between liberation theology and its critics. Where the polarization of positions has led to an impasse and further discussion has been rendered virtually impossible, this chapter will propose a way to reopen the dialogue.

THREAT OF INNOVATION

At the time of its earliest arrival in North America, bold claims were made for liberation theology both by Latin American proponents and North American sympathizers. Such claims set forth the uniqueness of liberation theology's method (that is, "a new way of doing theology"), declared its significance for the church worldwide, and even designated liberation theology as a "prophetic" movement. Such extraordinary claims were met with skepticism by many North American theologians. While every form of innovation meets with resistance from those holding well-established positions, this reaction was exaggerated from the very start by the magnitude of the claims made for liberation theology. This was made even more

---

1. Cf. Craig L. Nessan, *Orthopraxis or Heresy: The North American Theological Response to Latin American Liberation Theology* (Atlanta: Scholars, 1989), chapters 3 and 4.

poignant by liberation theology's appeal to Marxist analysis and daring to employ violence as a means of social and political change.

CRITICISM OF WESTERN ACADEMIC THEOLOGY

Liberation theology has been extremely critical of what it understands to be the deficiencies of Western "academic" theology. Where most modern theology has originated in the context of the European university, liberation theology has insisted on the particularity of the Latin American context for its position. Insofar as Western theology has become an academic discipline exercised by and for a professional elite, liberation theology would attend to the meaning of God for the poor people living in deprivation in the cities and on the land of Latin America. Where Western academic theology has valued an objective, unbiased methodology in addressing questions of intellectual interest, liberation theology insists on a method which is impassioned and partisan on behalf of a praxis to reduce human suffering and promote justice.

Those who have invested their lives in the pursuit of an intellectually responsible academic theology with its appropriate methods and modes of reflection can point to a long and respected tradition for their discipline.[2] To them the criticism by liberation theologians appears not only presumptuous but misguided in failing to appreciate the challenge which modern thought has presented to the very notion of God. Academic theology has been required in order to defend the very intelligibility of continuing to speak of God in the modern world.

Liberation theology's critique of academic theology has been further exacerbated by charging academic theologians themselves of providing the ideological framework by which an unjust international social order has been maintained. This criticism, derived from the sociology of knowledge, has set the stage for heated polemic. The social location of liberation theology differs dramatically from that of most professional theologians in the West.

---

2. Cf. Wolfhart Pannenberg, *Theology and the Philosophy of Science*, trans. Francis McDonagh (Philadelphia: Westminster, 1976) 228–96, and Gerhard Ebeling, *The Study of Theology*, trans. Duane Priebe (Philadelphia: Fortress, 1978).

The Vitality of Liberation Theology

REJECTING THE TENETS OF AMERICAN CIVIL RELIGION

Liberation theology has been unflinching in its criticism of the United States for economic, political, and military policies in support of authoritarian regimes unresponsive to the needs of the poor. This criticism, combined with liberation theology's use of certain Marxist categories (particularly that of class conflict) and its advocacy of socialism, stirs up an anti-communist sentiment which has deep roots in the American psyche.

Liberation theology has been radically iconoclastic in attacking the most cherished tenets of American civil religion.[3] The sociologist Robert Bellah has identified as an integral element of civil religion what he calls "the American taboo on socialism."[4] The connotations of "socialism" in American culture include images of the "foreign" and "alien"; of "collectivism" as opposed to the valued individualism of American belief; and of the atheistic and "anti-religious." Such a taboo on socialism was intensified during the decade of the 1980s by the prominence of the main themes of American civil religion under the influence of the Religious Right.[5]

Liberation theology's use of Marxist categories and advocacy of socialism as a project for the future of Latin America breaks this American taboo on socialism. By its criticism of the US role in contributing to social injustice in Latin America, it further assaults other basic tenets of American civil religion: that a unique covenant exists between God and America; that America is the "new Israel," the "chosen people," the "promised land," the "new Jerusalem";[6] that America is a "redeemer nation,"[7] a "beacon of light" to the poor; that America is beyond evil in the goodness

---

3. For an excellent summary of research on civil religion, see Andrew L. Pratt, "Religious Faith and Civil Religion: American Evangelism and the Vietnam War, 1964-1973" (PhD diss., The Southern Baptist Theological Seminary, 1988) 30-51.

4. Robert N. Bellah, *The Broken Covenant: American Civil Religion in Time of Trial* (New York: Seabury, 1975) 112-38.

5. Cf. Paul Johnson, "The Almost-Chosen People: Why America Is Different," First Annual Erasmus Lecture (Rockford: The Rockford Institute, 1985) 11-12.

6. Cf. Robert N. Bellah, "Civil Religion in America," in *Beyond Belief: Essays on Religion in a Post-Traditional World* (New York: Harper & Row, 1970) 168-89.

7. Cf. Ernest Lee Tuveson, *Redeemer Nation: The Idea of America's Millenial Role* (Chicago: University of Chicago Press, 1968).

of its purpose.⁸ The central assertion of liberation theology that God sides with the Latin American poor clashes with the assertion of civil religion that America is God's chosen people. Liberation theology's charge of American culpability for Latin American poverty contradicts civil religion's affirmation of American virtue. Not only does liberation theology question America's privileged place in the divine scheme of things but it dares to propose that God, in being partial to the poor, is against the policies of the United States. What is more, liberation theology dares to make its case with biblical arguments! For American civil religion, this is nothing other than heresy.

Liberation theology has raised a direct and aggressive challenge to the legitimacy of the tenets of American civil religion in a time when belief in these tenets have regained a high level of credibility in American society. Those North American theologians committed to the positive value of religion in providing a "sacred canopy" over American society have been most rigorous in their opposition to liberation theology.⁹

RIVAL TRAJECTORIES

Walter Brueggemann has argued that two trajectories of covenant tradition are prominent in the Old Testament, the Mosaic and the Davidic.¹⁰ While the Bible presents itself as one unified tradition, "critical scholarship, however, has now made it reasonable to assume that these two articulations of covenant are not only distinct but also came from very different centers of power and very different processes of tradition building."¹¹ The first of these trajectories, the Mosaic "tends to be a movement of protest which is situated among the disinherited and which articulates its theological vision in terms of a God who intrudes even

---

8. Robert N. Bellah, "Evil and the American Ethos," in *Sanctions for Evil: Sources of Social Destructiveness*, ed. Nevitt Stanford and Craig Comstalk (San Francisco: Jossey-Bass, 1971) 184–87.

9. The term "sacred canopy" comes from Peter L. Berger, *The Sacred Canopy: Elements of a Sociological Theory of Religion* (Garden City, NY: Doubleday, 1969). An elaborate defense of the idea that religion should provide a sacred canopy for American society is Richard John Neuhaus, *The Naked Square: Religion and Democracy in America* (Grand Rapids: Eerdmans, 1984).

10. Walter Brueggemann, "Trajectories in Old Testament Literature and the Sociology of Ancient Israel," *Journal of Biblical Literature* 98 (1979) 161–85.

11. Ibid., 161.

against seemingly impenetrable institutions and orderings. On the other hand, the Davidic tradition tends to be a movement of consolidation which is situated among the established and secure and which articulates its theological vision in terms of a God who faithfully abides and sustains on behalf of the present ordering."[12] Brueggemann proceeds to label these two distinct trajectories as the "liberation trajectory" and the "royal trajectory," respectively.

Could much of the debate for and against liberation theology be rooted in the differing biblical trajectories to which theologians appeal? Brueggemann himself suggests that this is the case by citing the differences between process hermeneutics and liberation hermeneutics. Liberation theology does appeal to a definite biblical trajectory running from the exodus through the seventh- and eighth-century Hebrew prophets to the proclamation of the Kingdom of God by Jesus. The critics of liberation theology have frequently appealed to a theology of creation consistent with the royal trajectory in their defense of established institutions.[13]

What is of particular importance in this paradigm is the recognition of how social location has impacted the development of the biblical tradition itself. The current polarization between a theology with royalist tendencies and liberation theology can be understood to be as old as the Old Testament traditions themselves. Contemporary theological rivals can each call upon a significant biblical trajectory to buttress their arguments. It does not suffice therefore to dismiss either the current defenders of the royal trajectory or the current representatives of the liberation trajectory by accusing them of "the mere rationalization of positions already taken."[14] This is due to the fact that the two conflicting biblical trajectories serve not only as a source for arguments in defense of a preconceived position but may themselves be creative of the conflicting positions in the first place. The royal trajectory fosters the development of a socially conservative theology which values stability and supports the established institutions while the liberation trajectory fosters a socially radical the-

---

12. Ibid., 162

13. Cf. Michael Novak, *Freedom With Justice: Catholic Social Thought and Liberal Institutions* (San Francisco: Harper & Row, 1984) 162–64.

14. This phrase comes from Schubert M. Ogden, "The Concept of a Theology of Liberation: Must a Christian Theology Today Be So Conceived?" in *The Challenge of Liberation Theology: A First World Response*, ed. Brian Mahan and L. Dale Richesin (Maryknoll, NY: Orbis, 1981) 134.

ology which values transformation and supports movements for social justice. The relationship between the origins of a particular theological option in one particular biblical trajectory and the warrants drawn from that particular biblical trajectory in defense of a particular contemporary theological option is thus a circular one.

Since there can be a tendency to make exclusive claims to divine sanction for one's own theological position based on either of these particular trajectories, the tendency toward polarization which characterizes the current discussion of liberation theology appears inherent to the Bible itself. The decisive arguments therefore cannot be solely based upon appeals to biblical authority. Appeals to biblical texts must be accompanied by the explanation of historical context—both the original one and the contemporary one—in the course of interpretation. The impasse of polarization can in part be dismantled by recognizing the complexity of the hermeneutical process in which all appeals to Scripture take place.

DIFFERENCES OF SUBSTANCE

Only when the foregoing issues have been cleared away can one begin to address the more substantive differences which appear to separate liberation theology and its critics. Significant matters do require clarification by liberation theologians, particularly questions such as these:[15]

1. What is the philosophical basis of liberation theology?
2. How does liberation theology articulate its method?
3. What is the theological anthropology of liberation theology?
4. How does liberation theology understand the meaning of salvation/liberation?

Of the many criticisms leveled against liberation theology, these four emerge as the most substantive questions.

Liberation theology has strongly emphasized praxis, criticizing academic theology for its abstraction. Is it possible, however, to entirely avoid philosophical underpinnings? Several North American theologians have charged that liberation theology owes too much to Marx. It would be constructive for liberation theologians to clarify their philosophical basis—for example, Juan Luis Segundo's use of Teilhard or Clodovis Boff's debt to Thomism.

15. Cf. Nessan, *Orthopraxis or Heresy*, 391–401.

The Vitality of Liberation Theology

In terms of method, liberation theology needs to further demonstrate the ways in which its theological vision establishes checks and balances upon its chosen praxis. What is the relationship between social analysis and theological vision in liberation theology? It has been charged that theology does little more than provide ideological justification for a predetermined course of action. For instance, against the charge that it is prone prematurely to adopt violence as a means of social change, liberation theology would do well to demonstrate how its grounding in the Christian traditions shapes its praxis. Whereas many outside the movement equate liberation theology with revolution, the symbiotic relationship between the basic Christian communities and liberation theology needs to be clearly elaborated.

The theological anthropology of liberation theology has been called into question by those who believe it fails to take human sinfulness into account sufficiently and seriously. On the one hand, this charge appears ironic in that liberation theology has made a major contribution toward analyzing the sinfulness of political and economic structures. On the other hand, many charge that liberation theology is overly optimistic in its estimate of human possibilities, particularly the possibilities of the poor. What role does the notion of sin play for liberation theology? How does one articulate the reality of human sinfulness without undermining the entire liberation project? Liberation theology must express the need for the present political and economic structures to be radically altered without surrendering a realistic understanding of human hubris.

In a parallel way, liberation theology has been accused of confusing salvation with historical progress. For example, the contrast between a Protestant understanding of the gospel as a matter of "justification by grace through faith" appears to be substantially different from liberation theology's insistence upon the gospel as "good news for the poor." Liberation theology, as it has begun to do already, must further elaborate the connection it sees between salvation in personal terms and salvation as social reality. The biblical notion of *shalom* provides one important foundation for this discussion.

Substantive issues like these do require further clarification in the conversation between liberation theology and its critics. Before it is possible, however, to carry on a constructive dialogue regarding such substantive issues, it is necessary to overcome the the extreme polarization of opinions within the North American debate over liberation theology.

Dynamics of Polarization

BEYOND POLARIZATION

Polarization feeds on certainty—certainty about the truth of one's own position and the falsehood of the position of one's theological opponent. In the controversy surrounding liberation theology, there is an urgent need for critical thought, which will assist in "de-ideologizing" not only the position of the opponent but especially one's own position.[16] While the effort to de-ideologize one's own position may be ill-suited to the maintenance of the polemical spirit often reigning in contemporary political discourse, it may be more appropriate to the arena of theological discourse.

A constructive approach in transcending the impasse of polarization would include two complementary moves. First, there is a need for a *critical appreciation* of the countervailing position. Such critical appreciation begins with an authentic encounter with the fundamental logic and arguments of the other position and a genuine attempt to understand it on its own terms. This requires the interpreter to make the same kind of effort at bridging the hermeneutical gap between her/his own context and that of liberation theology as is made at bringing the hermeneutical gap between her/his own context and that of an ancient text. A similar effort would be expected of liberation theologians in their interpretation of "academic" theology. Too often the reciprocating malediction between liberation theologians and critics has been based more on caricature than on a fair representation of the other's arguments.

A second move which could lead beyond the impasse of polarization involves the application of *self-criticism*. Critical thought does not begin and end with criticism of the arguments of others. Critical thought must also, if not primarily, be directed at one's own arguments. As Trutz Rendtorff has written regarding the scientific character of theology, ". . . the critical meaning of science is not attainable without the ethos of the scientific method which consists of being critical not only and not primarily over against 'others' but in relationship to one's own standpoint."[17] It is the absence of such self-critical thought which has marred the North American discussion of liberation theology and contributed to excessive polarization. The impasse of polarization can only be dismantled given a

---

16. The proposal of Schubert M. Ogden, *The Point of Christology* (San Francisco: Harper & Row, 1982) 3–96 and 164–68, regarding "de-ideologizing" deserves careful consideration as an essential component of theological method.

17. Trutz Rendtorff, *Ethik: Grundelemente, Methodologie und Konkretionen einer ethischen Theologie* (Stuttgart: Kohlhammer, 1980) 1:29 (my translation).

mutual commitment to both critical appreciation of the arguments of the other and self-criticism of one's own position.

In the context of Latin American poverty and the cry for a praxis that addresses the root causes of economic injustice, liberation theology deems other kinds of theology inadequate, if not diversionary. It is to be hoped that liberation theologians have learned to take seriously the most significant arguments set forth by North American theologians in criticism of its positions. At the same time, there needs to be far deeper understanding on the part of many North American theologians about the differentness of context in which liberation theology has originated and its validity in that context.

Liberation theology is a form of advocacy scholarship on behalf of the Latin American poor, which is deeply rooted in the Christian tradition. In their identification with the poor, liberation theologians, motivated by the gospel message, have attempted to construct a theological program that can lead to an increase in justice in Latin American social, economic, political, and ecclesial structures. If theologians in the North do not agree with the theological method, formulations, or praxis advocated by liberation theology, they should at least be challenged to recognize the difference in context in which liberation theology has arisen and reexamine the contextual nature of their own theology. They can, furthermore, be challenged to broaden their understanding of "reality" by discovering the reality of extreme poverty and social injustice, which have rarely in the past been adequately addressed by theology.[18]

On numerous occasions those North American theologians, missionaries, clergy, and lay persons who have immersed themselves in the Latin American context and who have experienced firsthand the situation of the Latin American poor have come to a new estimation of the validity of Latin American liberation theology. To those who have not yet been able to envision the context to which liberation theology seeks to respond, liberation theologians extend the invitation for them to come and see for themselves.

---

18. Cf. Trutz Rendtorff, "Universalität oder Kontextualität der Theologie: Eine 'europäische' Stellungnahme," *Zeitschrift für Theologie und Kirche* 74 (1977) 243–45.

9

How Social Is the Gospel?

ONE OF THE MOST provocative and, for many critics, questionable claims of Latin American liberation theology has been its application of the gospel to what it names "social sinfulness." Liberation theologians argue that the gospel of Jesus Christ must in our time address the social and political problems of hunger, substandard medical care, exploitative working relations, inadequate housing, and inhuman living conditions. For them the gospel reveals that such conditions are not the will of God but instead the consequence of exploitative political, economic, and legal structures. The salvation engendered by the gospel is integral, addressing sinfulness not only on the level of the individual but also that of society. Liberation theologians discover biblical warrant for this understanding of the gospel as they interpret the meaning of the exodus, the message of the prophets, and the concern of Jesus for the poor.[1]

Gustavo Gutiérrez articulates succinctly liberation theology's affirmation of the gospel's social dimension: "We mean that the annunciation of the Gospel, precisely insofar as it is a message of total love, has an inescapable political dimension, because it is addressed to people who live within a fabric of social relationships, which, in our case, keep them in a subhuman condition."[2] Gutiérrez is acutely aware of how this understanding is susceptible to the charge of "humanizing," "temporalizing," or "politicizing" the gospel.[3] He warns, however, that non-recognition of the

---

1. See Jon Sobrino, *Christology at the Crossroads: A Latin American Approach*, trans. John Drury (Maryknoll, NY: Orbis, 1978) 50–61, for an explication of how Jesus' proclamation of God's kingdom addresses both the personal and social dimensions of sin.

2. Gustavo Gutiérrez, *A Theology of Liberation: History, Politics, and Salvation*. trans. and ed. Caridad Inda and John Eagleson (Maryknoll, NY: Orbis, 1973) 270.

3. Cf. ibid., 270–72.

gospel's social and political impact has resulted in the use of the Christian message to protect privileged interest in preserving the status quo.

To guard against the gospel's "submersion into the purely historical realm," a new spirituality must emerge, "the new preaching of a Christian message which is incarnated—not lost—in our here and now."[4] While there is risk involved in such an approach, the living proclamation of the gospel within the context of the poor "will indicate that in every achievement of brotherhood and justice among men there is a step toward total communion. By the same token, it will indicate the incomplete and provisional character of any and every human achievement."[5] The gospel of Jesus Christ is made real in specific achievements of justice, though within the course of human history such realizations are always provisional, never final.

The insistence upon the social impact of the gospel made by liberation theology has been challenged on many fronts. *The Hartford Declaration* set the tone for this criticism of liberation theology when its tenth, eleventh, and twelfth themes declared the following as "false and debilitating to the Church's life and work":[6]

> Theme 10: The world must set the agenda for the Church. Social, political, and economic programs to improve the quality of life are ultimately normative for the Church's mission in the world.

> Theme 11: An emphasis on God's transcendence is at least a hindrance to, and perhaps incompatible with, Christian social concern and action.

> Theme 12: The struggle for a better humanity will bring about the kingdom of God.

One of the authors and signers of *The Hartford Declaration*, Richard John Neuhaus, stridently criticized liberation theology in numerous publications for politicizing the gospel and reducing the kingdom of God to an historically imminent category.[7]

---

4. Ibid., 271.

5. Ibid., 272

6. *The Hartford Declaration*, in *Theology Today* 32 (1975) 94.

7. Cf. Richard John Neuhaus, "Liberation as Program and Promise: On Refusing to Settle for Less," *Currents in Theology and Mission* 2 (1975) 90–99, 152–58.

How Social Is the Gospel?

Other theologians applying this criticism to liberation theology have included Michael Novak, James V. Schaal, and Carl E. Braaten.[8] For example, Braaten writes:

> In liberation theology the "gospel" represents the ideal state of affairs, which hopefully will come about some day and for which we ought to fight with all our might and main. The gospel is captured by ideology. We hear about the *demands* of the gospel which prescribe for Christians the kind of liberating praxis to which they ought to commit themselves. The future kingdom comes about through a synergism of divine grace and good works, in this case the right kind of political praxis.[9]

The very gospel which Gutiérrez claims must include the political dimension is, in the estimation of these critics, reduced to the political. Both the transcendent origin of the gospel and the eschatological fulfillment of the gospel are short-changed.

This criticism of liberation theology has become the focus of debate not only among theologians but also within wider circles of the church. Among Roman Catholics, the *Instruction on Certain Aspects of the "Theology of Liberation*," issued in 1984 by the Sacred Congregation for the Doctrine of the Faith, ignited an intense discussion of the legitimacy of liberation theology's interpretation of the gospel. Within the Lutheran Church, a question was raised regarding the propriety of employing funds from the Hunger Appeal for advocacy within the political process.[10] The question about the social dimension of the gospel is one with manifold consequences for the self-understanding and mission of the church.

The conflict between the liberationist interpretation of the gospel and its critics can be examined from numerous angles. One key issue involves how adequately the critics have understood the actual position of liberation theologians like Gutiérrez. Even more crucial is to evaluate how adequately their positions express what the New Testament means by euaggelion ("good news"). The purpose of this chapter is more modest,

---

8. See Michael Novak, *Will It Liberate? Questions about Liberation Theology* (Mahwah, NJ: Paulist, 1986); James V. Schaal, *Liberation Theology in Latin America* (San Francisco: Ignatius, 1982); and Carl E. Braaten, *The Flaming Center: A Theology of the Christian Mission* (Philadelphia: Fortress, 1977) 148–58.

9. Carl E. Braaten, *Principles of Lutheran Theology* (Philadelphia: Fortress, 1983) 107.

10. For example, Robert Benne, "Reconnect with the Christian Core," *The Lutheran* 2 (1989) 8.

however. Here we will examine four other twentieth-century answers to the question, how social is the gospel? The viewpoints of Walter Rauschenbusch, Karl Barth, Gustaf Wingren, and Schubert Ogden can shed additional perspective on this conflict.

WALTER RAUSCHENBUSCH

The name of Walter Rauschenbusch has in time become virtually synonymous with the social gospel movement of the late nineteenth and early twentieth centuries. Rauschenbusch shaped his theology of the social gospel according to his experience as a minister at the edge of Hell's Kitchen in New York City. In his final book, *A Theology for the Social Gospel*, Rauschenbusch argued for the necessity of a social gospel to address the sinfulness of the social order that is commensurate with the individualistic gospel which addresses the sinfulness of individual heart.[11] Such a gospel Rauschenbusch grounded in "the Hebrew faith which Jesus himself held."[12] When Jesus proclaimed the kingdom of God, he intended a "higher social order in which new ethical standards would become practicable."[13] Under the process of the Hellenization of Christianity, alien influence transformed this social gospel by making it individualistic. The ethical content of the kingdom of God for society was set aside in this process.

Rauschenbusch sought not to negate the importance of salvation for the individual but rather to incorporate it within the larger horizon of the social gospel.[14] Operating with a definition of sin as selfishness, Rauschenbusch described the conversion of the sinner from self-centeredness to concern for the neighbor. Insofar as Jesus identified himself with the hungry, naked, and lonely ones (Matt 25:31–46), the Christian needs to stand in solidarity with these neighbors in particular.

Rauschenbusch also raised the significance of the social gospel in countering what he called "super-personal social forces," for example, the negative effects which he perceived to derive from capitalism.[15] The law of

---

11. See Walter Rauschenbusch, *A Theology for the Social Gospel* (Nashville: Abingdon, 1945) 5.

12. Ibid., 24.

13. Ibid.

14. Ibid., 95–109.

15. Ibid., 110–17.

Christ can empower not only individuals but even states to turn from the motives of selfishness and greed to those of altruism and equity:

> The salvation of the super-personal beings is by coming under the law of Christ. The fundamental step of repentance and conversion for professions and organizations is to give up monopoly power and the incomes derived from legalized extortion, and to come under the law of service, content with a fair income for honest work. The corresponding step in the case of governments and political oligarchies, both in monarchies and in capitalistic semi-democracies, is to submit to real democracy. Therewith they step out of the kingdom of Evil into the kingdom of God.[16]

It is the function of the church to bring this social gospel to bear upon both individuals and super-personal beings (that is, organizations, businesses, and states).

The theological conviction at the heart of Rauschenbusch's social gospel is the kingdom of God. Where the kingdom of God is restored to the central place it held in the teachings of Jesus, the social gospel will be a dynamic force in transforming individuals, the church, and the entire social order into a community ordered by the will of God.

> Since love is the supreme law of Christ, the kingdom of God implies a progressive reign of love in human affairs. We can see its advance wherever the free will of love supersedes the use of force and legal coercion as a regulative of the social order. This involves the redemption of society from political autocracies and economic oligarchies; the substitution of redemptive for vindictive penology; the abolition of constraint through hunger as part of the industrial system; and the abolition of war as the supreme expression of hate and the completest cessation of freedom.[17]

History progresses by proximate realization of the kingdom until the hour of history's completion.

KARL BARTH

Perhaps no twentieth-century theologian reacted so critically to turn-of-the-century liberal theology (of which Rauschenbusch could be cited as a major example) than Karl Barth. Nevertheless, although grounded upon

---

16. Ibid., 117.
17. Rauschenbusch, *Theology for the Social Gospel*, 142–43.

a significantly different line of argumentation, Barth also clearly defended the impact of the gospel on the social-political sphere.

In his seminal essay, "Gospel and Law," Barth reversed the traditional order of these two theological categories.[18] He did so in order to stress the priority of God's word of gospel. The content of this gospel, for Barth, is the grace God has revealed to humankind in Jesus Christ. This gospel works to counter human sinfulness, which Barth typifies as autocracy and godlessness, human aversion and flight from the goodness of God's grace.

It is in linking the law of God to this gospel that Barth made provision for the social dimension within his understanding of the gospel. Barth's concise expression of the relationship between gospel and law is ". . . the Law is nothing else than the necessary *form of the Gospel*, whose content is grace."[19]

For Barth, the law functions as an indicative arising out of the gospel. God's law, known as divine gift, is comprehensible only to those who have already encountered the gospel of grace shown to humanity in Jesus Christ. The truth that Jesus Christ has already fulfilled the law opens up the possibility not only of human belief in Jesus Christ but even the possibility of human obedience and conformity to God's law. Such obedience and conformity to God's law is nothing less than the work and gift of the Holy Spirit.

The law of God emerging from the gospel is not only for individuals but inherently political. For Barth, as for Rauschenbusch, the New Testament phrase "the kingdom of God," insofar as it describes *a kingdom*, is filled with political ramifications.[20] The fullest description of the political nature of the gospel of the kingdom is located in Barth's essay "The Christian Community and the Civil Community":

> The gospel which proclaims the king and the kingdom that is now hidden but will one day be revealed is political from the very outset, and if it is preached to real (Christian and non-Christian) men on the basis of a right interpretation of the Scriptures it will necessarily be prophetically political. Explications and applications of its political content in an unmistakable direction will inevitably take

---

18. Karl Barth, "Gospel and Law," trans. A. M. Hall, in *Community, State, and Church: Three Essays*, ed. Will Herberg (Gloucester, MA: Peter Smith, 1968) 71–100.

19. Ibid., 80.

20. Karl Barth, "Church and State," trans. G. Ronald Howe, in *Community, State, and Church*, 124.

place (whether in direct or indirect illumination of the political problems of the day) where the Christian community is gathered together in the service of this gospel. Whether this happens or not will depend on the preachers, but not only on them. It is a bad sign when Christians are frightened by "political" sermons—as if Christian preaching could be anything but political. And if it were not political, how would it show that it is the salt and the light of the world? The Christian Church that is aware of its political responsibility will demand political preaching; and it will interpret it politically even if it contains no direct references to politics.[21]

The background for Barth's exposition of the political nature of the gospel is his own involvement in the Confessing Church movement in opposition to the ideology and politics within Hitler's Germany. It was Barth's contention that the church has the responsibility to be the model and prototype of an authentic state. This role of the church (vis-à-vis the state) is echoed in the fifth thesis from the *Barmen Theological Declaration*: "The Church acknowledges the benefaction of this divine ordinance with a thankful, reverent heart. It reminds men of God's kingdom, God's Commandment and justice, and thereby the responsibility of governors and governed alike. It trusts and obeys the power of the Word by which God sustains all things."[22]

The gospel, according to Barth, contains within itself the precepts of the law which can properly order all of life, including the social-political order. It is the task of the church to make witness in word and deed to the standards of God's law by which the political order is measured. That God speaks to humanity at all, whether as gospel or as law, is in itself grace.

GUSTAF WINGREN

The Swedish theologian Gustaf Wingren conceived the relationship between law and gospel to be radically different from Barth. In fact, Wingren's understanding of law and gospel was formulated in intentional opposition to Barth's proposal.[23] Wingren defended the more traditional ordering of law, then gospel—with a strict distinguishing between the

---

21. Karl Barth, "The Christian Community and the Civil Community," in *Community, State, and Church*, 184-85.

22. Quoted in ibid., 189.

23. Cf. Gustaf Wingren, *Theology in Conflict: Nygren, Barth, Bultmann*, trans. Eric H. Wahlstrom (Philadelphia: Muhlenberg, 1958).

function of each.[24] Basing this distinction upon the theology of Martin Luther, Wingren developed the category of law as the proper arena for a discussion of politics. God rules the political order, Christians and non-Christians alike, through the power of the law. The demand of God for justice is knowable to all people through the proper use of reason. In its first (or civil) use, the law structures human society, compelling obedience under fear of punishment. Just laws, enacted by the state, serve God's purpose of ordering civil society. In its second (or theological) use, the law points out the inability of perfect human obedience to the divine will. The sinner stands accused by God for all shortcomings under the measurement of the law. Again, Wingren held that the law, both in its civil and theological functions, is applicable to all persons apart from any encounter with the gospel. It is through created human reason that politics operates to enact laws for the governing of human affairs apart from any unique Christian contribution.

The function of the gospel, by contrast, is to restore those accused by the law of God to new life: "This Gospel is the kerygma which was preached in all the world after the resurrection, and for those who hear and accept it, it is both life—resurrection—and death—the putting to death of the old nature. . . . The Gospel as the good news of the forgiveness of sins is a word preached in the face of sin and the dominion of law throughout the world."[25] This gospel is the new and different work which God has brought to pass through the death and resurrection of Jesus Christ.

Does Wingren see any relationship between the gospel and politics? Yes, in a twofold way. The first aspect is quite indirect, working through the individual who has been justified by the Christian gospel. The individual who trusts in the redemption of God in Jesus Christ has been freed from self-concern and for genuine concern for the neighbor. The second aspect is through the collective engagement of Christians in the political arena, according to the civil use of the law, where love for the neighbor finds expression in the structures of society:

---

24. For the following, see Gustaf Wingren, *Creation and Law*, trans. Ross Mackenzie (Philadelphia: Muhlenberg, 1958).

25. Gustaf Wingren, *Gospel and Church*, trans. Ross Mackenzie (Philadelphia: Fortress, 1964) 111.

> The sphere in which a distinction is made between the demands made upon us by our fellow-men is not primarily parliament, government, or other legislative organ, but the relationship which the Christian has to his neighbor, that is to say in a relatively personal relationship which will vary in each case. Political matters are a special instance of this basic norm and a democratic society broadens the *mise en scene* by giving us more neighbors, but it is still the same reality with which we are dealing.[26]

Whereas the relationship of the gospel to politics is indirect, depending primarily on the individual's chosen expression of neighbor love, the relationship of the law to politics is most direct. All persons, including Christians, are under the mandate of God to establish just laws. According to Wingren, no legal system is absolute but each system requires constant revision under the criterion of love for the neighbor. This is especially urgent in view of the disparity between rich and poor nations in the modern world.[27]

SCHUBERT M. OGDEN

The theology of Schubert M. Ogden has been deeply influenced by Rudolf Bultmann, process thought, and, in his later career, the challenge of liberation theology. For Ogden, the central Christian doctrine requiring clarification in contemporary theology is the doctrine of God. It is through a twofold reformulation of the doctrine of God as Redeemer and Emancipator that Ogden attempted to solve the relationship between the gospel and the social-political relevance of the Christian faith.

Ogden, like Wingren, drew from the theology of Luther in seeking to understand the relationship of the gospel to things political. Ogden, however, drew exclusively from Luther's treatise *The Freedom of a Christ* in his elaboration of the two types of freedom in which the Christian exists, freedom "from" and freedom "for."[28] Ogden criticized the theologies of liberation for confusing these "two essentially different though closely

---

26. Ibid., 217.

27. Gustaf Wingren, *Creation and Gospel: The New Situation in European Theology* (New York: Mellen, 1979) 120–24.

28. Schubert M. Ogden, *Faith and Freedom: Toward a Theology of Liberation* (Nashville: Abingdon, 1979) 58–62.

related, forms of liberation."²⁹ Ogden's formulation of their correct relationship reads as follows:

> ... faith in God is indeed the existence of freedom in the twofold sense that it is both existence *in* freedom and existence *for* freedom. Because faith is utter trust in God's love as well as utter loyalty to him and his cause, it is both the negative freedom *from* all things and the positive freedom *for* all things—to love and serve them by so speaking and acting as to respond to all their creaturely needs. In this respect faith is existence in freedom, and so a *liberated* existence—an existence liberated by God's redeeming love. But because faith is utter loyalty to God and his cause as well as utter trust in him, it is also existence *for* freedom, and so also a *liberating* existence—an existence devoted to so bearing witness to God's love by all that we say and do as to optimize the limits of others' freedom in whatever ways this can be done.³⁰

The human being is passive with regard to the accomplishment of the first type of freedom. Here one is fully dependent upon the prerogative of God's redeeming love. With regard to the second form of freedom, however, the human being becomes activated by God's love and God's initiative to work for the liberation of all those who are unfree. Such unfreedom includes social-political bondage which calls forth political engagement.³¹

Ogden grounded this distinction between freedom "from" and freedom "for" in a reinterpretation of the doctrine of God. As Redeemer, God establishes the foundation of human freedom "from bondage to sin, as well as from the bondage of transience and death."³² This work of redemption is God's work alone, salvation by grace received through faith. As Emancipator, however, God invites human participation in extending "salvation" (not redemption) to all people. For Ogden, "the most important way in which we participate in God's work of emancipation is to labor for fundamental social and cultural change—the kind of structural or systematic change in the very order of society and culture that is clearly necessary if each and every person is to be the active subject of his or her

---

29. Ibid., 36.
30. Ibid., 64.
31. Cf. Schubert M. Ogden, *The Point of Christology* (San Francisco: Harper & Row, 1982) 166–68.
32. Ogden, *Faith and Freedom*, 87.

history instead of merely its passive object."³³ The gospel is related to the social-political dimension, according to Ogden, in the same way God's redemptive work is related to God's emancipatory work. Both are of God; both are necessary. Yet the two are necessarily distinguishable.

HOW SOCIAL IS THE GOSPEL?

In *The Power of the Poor in History*, Gutiérrez rehearsed the agony of nineteenth-century liberal theology having sold its birthright in forgetfulness of the poor. Twentieth-century theologians—from Barth to Tillich—sought to redress this malady, perhaps none so incisively as Bonhoeffer in his *Letters and Papers from Prison*: "God lets himself be pushed out of the world and on to the cross. He is weak and powerless in the world, and that is precisely the way, the only way, in which he is with us and helps us. Matthew 8:17 makes it quite clear that Christ helps us, not by virtue of his omnipotence, but by virtue of his weakness and suffering."³⁴

Gutiérrez comments that "Bonhoeffer's own direct and cruel experience of suffering, as victim of the Nazi repression, and martyr—witness—of God's helpless love in the political condition of his time, was a factor of vital importance in molding this perception."³⁵ The entire generation of theologians that underwent the spasms of twentieth-century violence and oppression in this way laid foundations for the emergence of a suffering theology from the context of poverty in Latin America.

What conclusions can be drawn from the thought of the four featured theologians for the criticisms posed against liberation theology's explication of the gospel? First, recalling the positions of those as diverse as Rauschenbusch and Barth should alleviate the accusation that liberation theologians have introduced an innovation by incorporating the social-political dimension into their understanding of the gospel. Numerous other modern theologians (for example, Albrecht Ritschl), following the lead of Kant, have held the ethical dimension of Christianity to be of paramount importance, also with social and political impulses.

Second, there is a significant divergence of opinion regarding the correct interpretation of the New Testament idea of the "kingdom of

---

33. Ibid., 93–94.

34. Dietrich Bonhoeffer, as quoted in Gustavo Gutierrez, *The Power of the Poor in History*, trans. Robert R. Barr (Maryknoll: Orbis, 1983) 180.

35. Ibid.

God" in this discussion. Those who stress the gospel's social dimension emphasize it as *a kingdom* through which God is ruling *already* in the present. These theologians (Rauschenbusch, Barth, Gutiérrez) are willing to employ the kingdom of God as an *imminent* category. Those who criticize the gospel's social dimension point, instead, to the kingdom's *future and eschatological* character. They argue that the kingdom is future and transcendent, totally subject to the divine initiative. There is no adequate theological consensus regarding the "already-not yet" character of God's kingdom.

Third, each of the four theologians sheds light on the debate between liberation theology and its critics. In comparison to Rauschenbush, liberation theology is far more nuanced and cautious regarding a temporal realization of the kingdom of God. Gutiérrez, for example, while stressing the social-political relevance of the gospel, repeatedly indicates that all gains in justice remain "incomplete and provisional." Rauschenbusch seldom attached such reservations to his expectation of the growth of the kingdom.

In the theology of Barth, it is God who is active in the capacity as divine politician. Human politics are to reflect the political priorities of God's kingdom. Such a position can provide a constant check and criterion on all human politics, while at the same time insisting upon God's own involvement in politics. Liberation theology, with reference to the biblical narrative, shares to a degree Barth's understanding of God as politician. Liberation theologians, however, go much farther than Barth by seeking to mediate divine politics into the complexities of Latin American society. In attempting such mediation, liberation theology opens itself to the criticism of politicizing the gospel. Without such concrete mediation, however, political theology remains mere rhetoric.

Of the four theologians examined in this article, the critics of liberation theology have most in common with Wingren. For example, Neuhaus and Braaten share Wingren's insistence upon a clear distinction between law and gospel. For them, while engagement in politics is important, political involvement belongs to the realm of the law operating through human reason. The gospel does not speak directly to this realm but rather indirectly through the justification of individual sinners who are freed to love their neighbors. One expression of neighbor love is the political.

Wingren's understanding of the gospel differs notably from that of liberation theology. There can be no agreement regarding the social relevance of the gospel as long as there remains such critical differences in defining the gospel itself. Ogden, by differentiating between the gospel as redemption and as emancipation, offers a proposal which seems to give balanced consideration to the arguments of both liberation theology and its critics. By distinguishing between a passive and an active moment within God's salvific work, redemption is guarded as the work of God alone while inviting human participation in God's emancipating work of increasing freedom for those oppressed by the chains of injustice.

Once again, the central question involves the very definition of the gospel. Does the gospel itself pertain only to the passive moment Ogden names redemption? Or can the active moment, which he names emancipation, also be incorporated into what is meant by the gospel? The division between liberation theology and its critics regarding the question of how social is the gospel can only be bridged by addressing this question. Liberation theology joins ranks with other theologians—Barth, Tillich, Bonhoeffer, Moltmann—in pressing for an affirmation of the inherently social character of the gospel.

Conclusion

The Vitality of Liberation Theology

LIBERATION THEOLOGY BEGINS WITH the fact of desperate poverty as the fundamental scandal it seeks to redress. While under certain, circumscribed conditions poverty can be claimed as a spiritual blessing among those whose lives have been simplified of the many distractions and contradictions that prevent them from practicing unencumbered faith in God and discipleship, the existential reality of life in extreme poverty should not be romanticized. Although I have experienced many times the spiritual blessing of radical hospitality among the company of poor people in Latin America and elsewhere in our world, the fact remains that poverty is a curse that stunts human fulfillment and a challenge that demands structural transformation of society. Analyzing extreme poverty as the consequence of the dependency of economically distressed peoples upon the largesse of economic elites leads liberation theologians to advocate for the necessity of both global and local adjustments in fair access to and equitable distribution of food, water, land, health care, technology, employment, and other forms of wealth.

The contemporary crisis created by economic globalization presents unprecedented challenges to the vitality of liberation theology in Latin America. The economic structures contributing to extreme poverty seem even more intractable than they first appeared at the dawn of liberation theology. If the initial impulse giving rise to the emergence of liberation theology was the ugly fact of poverty and economic injustice, this reality has not changed in the intervening years. The need for a liberation theology, grounded in Scripture and the theological tradition, appears more urgent than ever before.

Duchrow and Hinkelammert have argued for the revitalization of dependency theory as a crucial resource for analyzing the globalized economy from the perspective of the poor.

Conclusion: The Vitality of Liberation Theology

> So today the First World is a great archipelago found everywhere on our planet, but surrounded by zones that cannot be integrated either socially or economically. Although this archipelago still lies particularly in the North, the relationship can no longer be understood as a North-South relationship. It can be designated, however, in terms of exclusion . . . Every human activity must now become capital and bear interest, so that investment-seeking capital can live: kindergartens, universities, health systems, energy utilities, roads, railways, the post office, telecommunications, and other means of communication, etc. . . . Even the police and legislation are to be transformed into capital investments.[1]

Such a reconceptualization of dependency theory, or some other more adequate economic theory, is imperative, if the reality of extreme poverty is to be taken with utmost seriousness as the point of departure and central concern for liberation theology. Otherwise, as analyzed by Ivan Petrella, the future of genuine liberation may lie with disciplines other than theology (economics, law, sociology, political science) that demonstrate a greater capacity to affect radical change in the lives of the poor.[2]

The examination of Latin American history by liberation theologians takes the "view from below." From the time of the colonial conquest to the present, the history of Latin America has been characterized by exploitation, oppression, and repression. Liberation theology articulates a "people's history" that tells a partisan account from the perspective of the indigenous and poor people who have had to cope with these realities. Since the emergence of Latin American liberation theology in the 1960s, theologians, pastors, priests, bishops, and laity, who are partisan to this stance, have raised a prophetic voice, speaking and acting in solidarity with the marginalized and poor, stirring them to claim their own dignity and agency.

Liberation theology is grounded in a reading of Scripture and an appropriation of the theological tradition that claims the biblical God as a God of justice—one who hears the cries of the poor, sends prophets to demand righteousness from the powerful, and empowers the people to act. The method of liberation theology is that of praxis. Embedded in the social realities of the poor, liberation theologians shout a dramatic "No!"

---

1. Ulrich Duchrow and Franz J. Hinkelammert, *Property for People, Not for Profit: Alternatives to the Global Tyranny of Capital*, trans. Elaine Griffiths et al. (New York: Zed, 2004) 146, 148.

2. Ivan Petrella, *Beyond Liberation Theology: A Polemic* (London: SCM, 2008) 148–50.

against the status quo. Drawing upon the social sciences, liberation theologians analyze the factors leading to poverty, drawing upon elements of Marxist analysis and appealing to dependency theory. This has been one of the most provocative and controversial moves on the part of liberation theology.

At the same time, liberation theology appeals to the justice trajectory in the Bible and to usable streams of the theological tradition to construct a movement for social transformation and justice. The theological claims of liberation theology feed practical engagement in changing the structures that hold the poor in bondage. The activism by members of the basic Christian communities represents the chief agency issuing from liberation theology. Because some liberation theologians have advocated the use of counter-violence against structural violence as a legitimate means for social change, liberation theology has sometimes come under severe criticism. North American and European reactions to liberation theology have been extremely polarized, ranging from staunch defense to absolute rejection. However, the social location of liberation theology, together with its appeal to major trajectories within Scripture, do not allow for easy dismissal of its core assertions.

Liberation theology has not been without blind spots. Liberation theologians were slow and hesitating in forging coalitions with black liberation theology and feminist theology from the First World.[3] However, in recent decades, liberation theology has expanded its horizons to incorporate alliances with other forms of contextual theology across the globe, sought to address structural sexism by adding *mujerista* perspectives, and also begun to integrate ecological justice as an essential dimension.[4] Moreover, liberation theologians have grown in their appreciation for and constructive references to previously overlooked indigenous religious traditions.[5]

---

3. Cf. the exchanges between Latin American, black, and feminist theologians in Sergio Torres and John Eagleson, eds., *Theology in the Americas* (Maryknoll, NY: Orbis, 1976).

4. Cf. Sergio Torres and John Eagleson, eds, *The Challenge of Basic Christian Communities: Papers from the International Ecumenical Congress of Theology, February 29–March 2, 1980, in São Paulo, Brazil* (Maryknoll, NY: Orbis, 1981); Ada María Isasi-Díaz, *En La Lucha/In the Struggle: Elaborating a Mujerista Theology*, 10th anniversary ed. (Minneapolis: Fortress, 2004); Leonardo Boff, *Cry of the Earth, Cry of the Poor*, trans. Phillip Berryman (Maryknoll, NY: Orbis, 1997).

5. Edward L. Cleary and Timothy J. Steigenga, eds., *Resurgent Voices in Latin America:*

Conclusion: The Vitality of Liberation Theology

At the end of the twentieth and beginning of the twenty-first centuries, several critical commentators ventured to declare the demise or "death" of liberation theology. Such claims, however, fail both to acknowledge the vitality of liberation perspectives in the Latin American context and to recognize the substantial ways Latin American liberation theology has changed irreversibly the very way theology is done across the globe. Within Latin America, the perspective of liberation theology continues to bring vitality to theological discourse and action in a context that remains in bondage to deeply embedded forms of oppression.[6]

In other contexts of oppression, Latin American liberation theology has served to catalyze and accompany the emergence of innovative contextual theologies advocating for radical structural changes: anti-apartheid theology in South Africa and Namibia, *Minjung* theology in Korea, *Dalit* theology in India, or Palestinian liberation theology.[7] In Europe and North America, the proposals of Latin American liberation theologians have transformed the discourse of systematic theology in decisive and profound ways. Not only progressive Protestant, but also Evangelical Protestant and Roman Catholic theologians have engaged with and incorporated crucial aspects of Latin American liberation theology into their own perspectives.[8] Representatives of this influence include Jürgen Moltmann and Johannes Baptist Metz in Germany, Douglas John Hall in Canada, and Rosemary Radford Ruether, John Cobb Jr., and David Tracy in the United States. Moreover, Latin American liberation theology has contributed to the reclaiming of latent themes in the theological

---

Indigenous Peoples, Political Mobilization, and Religious Change (New Brunswick: Rutgers University Press, 2004).

6. Ivan Petrella, ed., *Latin American Liberation Theology: The Next Generation* (Maryknoll, NY: Orbis, 2005).

7. John W. de Gruchy and Charles Villa-Vicencio, eds., *Apartheid Is a Heresy* (Grand Rapids: Eerdmans, 1983); Commission on Theological Concerns of the Christian Conference of Asia, ed., *Minjung Theology: People as the Subjects of History* (Maryknoll, NY: Orbis, 1983); Sathianathan Clarke, *Dalits and Christianity: Subaltern Religion and Liberation Theology* (Delhi: Oxford University Press, 1998); and Naim Stifan Ateek, *Justice and Only Justice: A Palestinian Theology of Liberation* (Maryknoll, NY: Orbis, 1989).

8. Craig L. Nessan, "Orthopraxis and Martyrdom: The Influence of Latin American Liberation Theology on Systematic Theology in Europe and the North America," in Paul Chung, Ulrich Duchrow, and Craig L. Nessan, *Liberating Lutheran Theology: Freedom for Justice and Solidarity with Others in a Global Context* (Minneapolis: Fortress, 2011) 53–67.

tradition, such as the theology of the cross.⁹ The contributions of Winston D. Persaud, Mary M. Solberg, David A. Brondos, and Vitor Westhelle are noteworthy among those who have reinterpreted the theology of the cross in relation to insights from liberation theology.

Vitor Westhelle has posed a critical question about the contributions of these varied liberation impulses in the postcolonial context: What, finally, do these subaltern voices share in common? Are they only unified by their opposition to the hegemony of colonialism and globalization as these have unfolded in the modern world? Or is there a deeper commonality that needs to be claimed? Westhelle writes:

> . . . the sublime task of theology is nothing but to consider and raise up the plea of those who are bent over by the weight of sin and oppression—the supplicants, the humiliated ones. The task of theology demands heeding to the voices of the voiceless, bringing to sight the invisible, lifting the downtrodden, the subalterns, for, down there, where they are, is where glory lies. This is the hybrid task of a subaltern and liberating theology today.[10]

The "hybridity" of a liberating theology crosses "national and ethnic frontiers" to represent "God's presence in a human that goes to such low depths into depravity as to encompass the whole of creation . . ."[11] To this enduring project liberation theologians have poured out their lifeblood.

This book articulates the core convictions and historical significance of liberation theology for the next generation. One can comprehend neither the turn to contextual theologies nor the insistence on social justice in contemporary theology without engaging the commitments of Latin American liberation theologians. For all of these reasons, Latin American liberation theology persists with vigor into the twenty-first century and will be recognized as a defining moment in theological history by future generations.

---

9. Craig L. Nessan, "'Thine Is the Kingdom, the Power, and the Glory': New Vistas for the Theology of the Cross," *Dialog* 50 (2011) 81–89.

10. Vitor Westhelle, *After Heresy: Colonial Practices and Post-Colonial Theologies* (Eugene, OR: Cascade, 2010) 163.

11. Ibid., 157.

Bibliography

Aguilar, Mario I. *The History and Politics of Latin American Theology*. 2 vols. London: SCM, 2007–2008.

Altmann, Walter. *Luther and Liberation: A Latin American Perspective*. Translated by Mary M. Solberg. Eugene: Wipf & Stock, 1992.

Alves, Rubem A. *A Theology of Human Hope*. St. Meinrad, IN: Abbey, 1975.

Batstone, David et al., editors. *Liberation Theologies, Postmodernity, and the Americas*. New York: Routledge, 1997.

Bevans, Stephen B. *Models of Contextual Theology*. Maryknoll, NY: Orbis, 1998.

Boff, Clodovis. *Theology and Praxis: Epistemological Foundations*. Translated by Robert R. Barr. Maryknoll, NY: Orbis, 1987.

Boff, Clodovis, and George V. Pixley. *The Bible, the Church, and the Poor*. Translated by Paul Burns. Maryknoll, NY: Orbis, 1989.

Boff, Leonardo. *Ecology and Liberation: A New Paradigm*. Translated by John Cumming. Maryknoll, NY: Orbis, 1995.

———. *Faith on the Edge: Religion and Marginalized Existence*. Translated by Robert R. Barr. San Francisco: Harper & Row, 1989.

———. *Holy Trinity, Perfect Community*. Translated by Phillip Berryman. Maryknoll, NY: Orbis, 1988.

———. *Jesus Christ Liberator: A Critical Christology for Our Time*. Translated by Patrick Hughes. Maryknoll, NY: Orbis, 1981.

———. *Trinity and Society*. Translated by Paul Burns. Maryknoll, NY: Orbis, 1988.

———. *When Theology Listens to the Poor*. Translated by Robert R. Barr. San Francisco: Harper & Row, 1988.

Boff, Leonardo, and Clodovis Boff. *Liberation Theology: From Dialogue to Confrontation*. Translated by Robert R. Barr. San Francisco: Harper & Row, 1986.

———. *Salvation and Liberation: In Search of a Balance between Faith and Politics*. Translated by Robert R. Barr. Maryknoll, NY: Orbis, 1984.

Brondos, David A. *Fortress Introduction to Salvation and the Cross*. Minneapolis: Fortress, 2007.

Brown, Robert McAfee. *Gustavo Gutiérrez: An Introduction to Liberation Theology*. Maryknoll, NY: Orbis, 1990.

———. *Kairos: Three Prophetic Challenges to the Church*. Grand Rapids: Eerdmans, 1990.

Cavanaugh, William T. *Torture and Eucharist: Theology, Politics, and the Body of Christ*. Malden, MA: Blackwell, 1998.

Chung, Paul S. *Christian Mission and a Diakonia of Reconciliation: A Global Reframing of Justification and Justice*. Minneapolis: Lutheran University Press, 2008.

———. *Public Theology in an Age of World Christianity: God's Mission as Word-Event*. New York: Palgrave Macmillan, 2010.

———. *The Spirit of God Transforming Life: The Reformation and Theology of the Holy Spirit*. New York: Palgrave Macmillan, 2009.

Bibliography

Chung, Paul S., Ulrich Duchrow, and Craig L. Nessan. *Liberating Lutheran Theology: Freedom for Justice and Solidarity with Others in a Global Context.* Minneapolis: Fortress, 2010.

Duchrow, Ulrich. *Alternatives to Global Capitalism: Drawn from Biblical History, Designed for Political Action.* Translated by Elizabeth Hicks et al. Heidelberg: Kairos Europa, 1998.

———. *Europe in the World System, 1492–1992: Is Justice Possible?* Translated by Keith Archer. Geneva: WCC, 1992.

Duchrow, Ulrich, and Franz Hinkelammert. *Property for People, Not for Profit: Alternatives to the Global Tyranny of Capital.* Translated by Elaine Griffiths et al. London: Zed, 2004.

Duchrow, Ulrich, and Gerhard Liedke. *Shalom: Biblical Perspectives on Creation, Justice, and Peace.* Geneva: WCC, 1989.

Dussel, Enrique, editor. *The Church in Latin America, 1492–1992.* Translated by Alan Neely. Maryknoll, NY: Orbis, 1992.

———. *Ethics and Community.* Translated by Robert R. Barr. Maryknoll: Orbis Books, 1988.

———. *A History of the Church in Latin America: Colonialism to Liberation (1492–1979).* Grand Rapids: Eerdmans, 1981.

Eagleson, John, editor. *Christians and Socialism: Documentation of the Christians for Socialism Movement in Latin America.* Translated by John Drury. Maryknoll, NY: Orbis, 1975.

Eagleson, John, and Philip Scharper, editors. *Puebla and Beyond: Documentation and Commentary.* Translated by John Drury. Maryknoll, NY: Orbis, 1979.

Ellacuría, Ignacio, and Jon Sobrino, editors. *Myterium Liberationis: Fundamental Concepts of Liberation Theology.* Maryknoll, NY: Orbis, 1993.

Ellis, Marc H., and Otto Maduro, editors. *The Future of Liberation Theology: Essays in Honor of Gustavo Gutiérrez.* Maryknoll, NY: Orbis, 1989.

Fabella, Virginia, and R. S. Sugirtharajah, editors. *The SCM Dictionary of Third World Theologies.* London: SCM, 2003.

Freire, Paulo. *Pedagogy of the Oppressed.* Translated by Myra Bergman Ramos. New York: Seabury, 1968.

González, Ondina E., and Justo L. González. *Christianity in Latin America.* Cambridge: Cambridge University Press, 2008.

Gutiérrez, Gustavo. *The Density of the Present: Selected Writings.* Maryknoll, NY: Orbis, 1999.

———. *The God of Life.* Translated by Matthew J. O'Connell. Maryknoll, NY: Orbis, 1991.

———. *Las Casas: In Search of the Poor of Jesus Christ.* Translated by Robert R. Barr. Maryknoll, NY: Orbis, 1993.

———. *The Power of the Poor in History.* Translated by Robert R. Barr. Maryknoll, NY: Orbis, 1983.

———. *A Theology of Liberation: History, Politics, and Salvation.* Translated and edited by Caridad Inda and John Eagleson. Maryknoll, NY: Orbis, 1988.

———. *The Truth Shall Make You Free: Confrontations.* Translated by Matthew J. O'Connell. Maryknoll, NY: Orbis, 1990.

———. *We Drink from Our Own Wells: The Spiritual Journey of a People.* Translated by Matthew J. O'Connell. Maryknoll, NY: Orbis, 1984.

Hall, Douglas J. *The Cross in Our Context: Jesus and the Suffering World*. Minneapolis: Fortress, 2003.
Hennelly, Alfred T. *Liberation Theologies: The Global Pursuit of Justice*. Mystic, CT: Twenty-Third Publications, 1995.
———, editor. *Liberation Theology: A Documentary History*. Maryknoll, NY: Orbis, 1990.
Howsam, Chris. *A Just Church: Twenty-First Century Liberation Theology in Action*. New York: Continuum, 2011.
Jennings, Theodore W., Jr. *Transforming Atonement: A Political Theology of the Cross*. Minneapolis: Fortress, 2009.
McGovern, Arthur F. *Liberation Theology and Its Critics: Toward an Assessment*. Maryknoll, NY: Orbis, 1989.
Míguez Bonino, José. *Doing Theology in a Revolutionary Situation*. Philadelphia: Fortress, 1975
———. *Toward a Christian Political Ethics*. Philadelphia: Fortress, 1983.
Miranda, José Porfirio. *Marx and the Bible: A Critique of the Philosophy of Oppression*. Translated by John Eagleson. Maryknoll, NY: Orbis, 1974.
Moe-Lobeda, Cynthia. *Healing a Broken World: Globalization and God*. Minneapolis: Fortress, 2002.
Nessan, Craig L. *Orthopraxis or Heresy: The North American Theological Response to Latin American Liberation Theology*. Atlanta: Scholars, 1989.
———. *Shalom Church: The Body of Christ as a Ministering Community*. Minneapolis: Fortress, 2010.
Persaud, Winston D. *The Theology of the Cross and Marx's Anthropology: A View from the Caribbean*. New York: Peter Lang, 1991.
Petrella, Ivan. *Beyond Liberation Theology: A Polemic*. London: SCM, 2008.
———, editor. *Latin American Liberation Theology: The Next Generation*. Maryknoll, NY: Orbis, 2005.
Richard, Pablo, et al. *The Idols of Death and the God of Life: A Theology*. Translated by Barbara E. Campbell and Bonnie Shepard. Maryknoll, NY: Orbis, 1983.
Rowland, Christopher, editor. *The Cambridge Companion to Liberation Theology*. Cambridge: Cambridge University Press, 1999.
Segundo, Juan Luis. *The Liberation of Dogma*. Translated by Phillip Berryman. Maryknoll, NY: Orbis, 1992.
———. *Liberation of Theology*. Translated by John Drury. Maryknoll, NY: Orbis, 1976.
Sigmund, Paul E. *Liberation Theology at the Crossroads: Democracy or Revolution?* New York: Oxford University Press, 1990.
Sobrino, Jon. *Christ the Liberator*. Translated by Paul Burns. Maryknoll, NY: Orbis, 2001.
———. *Jesus the Liberator: A Historical-Theological View*. Translated by Paul Burns and Francis McDonagh. Maryknoll, NY: Orbis, 1993.
———. *Where Is God? Earthquake, Terrorism, Barbarity, and Hope*. Translated by Margaret Wilde. Maryknoll, NY: Orbis, 2004.
Sobrino, Jon, and Ignacio Ellacuría, editors. *Systematic Theology: Perspectives from Liberation Theology*. Maryknoll, NY: Orbis, 1996.
Solberg, Mary M. *Compelling Knowledge: A Feminist Proposal for an Epistemology of the Cross*. Albany: State University of New York Press, 1997.
Tamez, Elsa. *The Amnesty of Grace: Justification by Faith from a Latin American Perspective*. Translated by Sharon H. Ringe. Nashville: Abingdon, 1993.

Bibliography

———. *Bible of the Oppressed*. Translated by Matthew J. O'Connell. Maryknoll, NY: Orbis, 1982.

Tombs, David. *Latin American Liberation Theology*. Boston: Brill, 2002.

Torres, Sergio, and John Eagleson, editors. *Theology in the Americas*. Maryknoll, NY: Orbis, 1976.

Trelstad, Marit, editor. *Cross Examinations: Readings on the Meaning of the Cross Today*. Minneapolis: Fortress, 2006.

Westhelle, Vitor. *After Heresy: Colonial Practices and Post-Colonial Theologies*. Eugene, OR: Cascade, 2010.

———. *The Scandalous God: The Use and Abuse of the Cross*. Minneapolis: Fortress, 2006.

Name Index

Allende, Salvador, 41, 43, 46
Altmann, Walter, *xi*, 91
Alves, Rubem, 30
Arns, Paulo Evaristo, 53
Assmann, Hugo, 36, 42, 48

Baggio, Sebastian, 47, 51
Banzer, Hugo, 43, 45
Barriero, Alvaro, 5, 99
Barth, Karl, *xi*, 136–39, 143–45
Baum, Gregory, 108
Belaguer, Joachin, 43
Bellah, Robert, 126
Bermudez, Moralez, 43
Bezerra de Melo, Almeri, 118
Boff, Clodovis, 118, 129
Boff, Leonardo, 58, 102, 106
Bonapart, Napoleon, 19
Bonhoeffer, Dietrich, *xi*, 143, 145
Borg, Marcus, 70
Braaten, Carl E., 135, 144
Brondos, David A., 150
Brueggemann, Walter, 127, 128
Bultmann, Rudolf, 141

Cardenal, Earnesto, 54, 62, 98
Carter, Jimmy, 44
Castro, Emilio, 30
Castro, Fidel, 24, 25
Chung, Paul S., *ii, iii, v, vii, xxii*
Clark, J. B., 22
Cobb Jr., John, 150
Colonnese, Louis, 45
Columbus, Christopher, 59
Cone, James H., *xiv*
Cousineau Adriance, Madeleine, 101
Cox, Harvey, 37

Crossan, John Dominic, 70

d'Escoto, Miguel, 54
Danker, Fredrick W., 74
Duchrow, Ulrich, *v*, 147
Dussel, Enrique, 4, 5, 123
Duvalier, Francois, 43

Ellacuría, Ignacio, 5, 56, 67, 103, 121

Foucauld, Charles de, 121
Freire, Paulo, 93, 94
Freud, Sigmund, 112

Galilea, Segundo, 31, 122
Gandhi, Mohandas, x, 122
Gera, Lucio, 31
Guevara, Che, *xiii*, 33
Gunder Frank, Andre, 115
Gutierrez, Gustavo, 2–5, 31, 40, 42, 58, 60, 78, 80–82, 90, 101, 106, 116–18, 133, 135, 143, 144

Hall, Douglas John, 149
Hart, John, 16
Hebblethwaite, Margaret, 103
Helder Camara, Dom, 118, 119, 122
Hellwig, Monika, 118
Hengsbach, Franz, 47
Hernandez Pico, Juan, 54
Hinkelammert, Franz, 147
Hitler, Adolf, 139

Johnson, Lyndon B., 44

Kant, Emmanuel, 143
Kennedy, John F., 23, 44

Name Index

King Jr., Martin Luther, x, xiii, 121, 122

Las Casas, Bartolomé de, xii, 18, 19, 60
Lenin, Vladimir, 111
Lernoux, Penny, 97
Lopez Trujillo, Alfonso, 39, 46–49, 51, 52
Luther, Martin, 91–92, 140, 141
Lorscheider, Aloisio, 49

Maritain, Jacques, 21
Martin, David, 60
Marx, Karl, x, xi, 79, 80, 84–86, 90, 91, 105, 108–10, 112–16, 129
McGovern, Arthur F., 107
Melano Couch, Beatriz, 89
Merton, Thomas, xiii
Metz, Johannes Baptist, 149
Miguez Bonino, Jose, 2–5, 30, 78, 87–90, 107, 109, 121,122
Moltmann, Jürgen, 144, 149
Moxnes, Halvor, 68, 69, 72

Nessan, Craig L., ix, x, xi, xv
Neuhaus, Richard John, 134, 144
Nietzsche, Friedrich, 112
Nixon, Richard, 44
Novak, Michael, 57, 135

Ogden, Shubert, xi, 136, 141–43, 145

Paz, Nestor, 25, 120
Pereira Ramalho, Jether, 97
Pérez Esquivel, Adolfo, 122
Peron, Juan, 43
Persaud, Winston D., 150
Petrella, Ivan, 1, 147
Pixley, George V., 1, 2
Pope John XXIII, 26, 27
Pope John Paul I, 50, 51
Pope John Paul II, 26, 50, 51, 57
Pope Paul VI, 37, 34, 95

Porfiro Miranda, José, 78, 84–87, 90, 114, 115

Radford Ruether, Rosemary, 150
Ratzinger, Joseph, 57, 106
Rauschenbush, Walter, xi, 144
Reagan, Ronald, 56
Rendtorff, Trutz, 131
Ritschl, Albrecht, 143
Rockefeller, John D., 44
Roldán Ortiga, Roque, 10
Romero, Oscar, 52

Santa Ana, Julio de, 30
Sandino, Augusto Cesar, 53, 54
Segundo, Juan Luis, 31, 78, 82–84, 90, 111, 120, 121, 129
Schaal, James V., 135
Schumpeter, Joseph, 22
Shaull, Richard, 28, 30, 117
Sobrino, Jon, 10, 56, 58, 103, 106
Solberg, Mary M., 150
Somoza Debyle, Anastasio, 53, 54
Stalin, Joseph, 110
Stroessner, Alfredo, 43

Teilhard de Chardin, Pierre, 83, 90, 129
Tillich, Paul, 146, 148
Tombs, David, 60, 61
Torres, Camilo, xiii, 25, 33, 120, 121
Tracy, David, 150
Truman, Harry S., 44

Vekemans, Roger, 46, 47, 49
Vidales, Raul, 97

Westhelle, Vitor, 150
Wingren, Gustav, xi, 136, 139–41, 144, 145

Zacchi, Cesare, 25
Zea, Leopold, 9

Subject Index

Academic theology, 125–27, 131
Advocacy scholarship, 132
Adveniat, 47
Amnesty International, 13
Atheism, 109–10

Barmen Declaration, 139
Base Communities, 15–16, 49, 58, 62, 93–104, 148

Capitalism, 114–15
Christendom, 21–22
Christians for Socialism, 37, 41–43, 47
Church and Society in Latin America (ISAL), 29–30, 32, 42
Civil religion, 126–27
Colonialism, 16–19, 147, 150
Congregation for the Doctrine of the Faith, 57–58, 102, 105, 135
Conscientization, 36, 93–94
Contextual theologies, xivf., 149
Critical appreciation, 131
Critiques of liberation theology, 133–35, 144–45
Cuban revolution, 24–25

Dangerous memory, 76–77
Dependency theory, 13, 42, 115–17, 147–48
Development theory, 22–24, 49

Economic globalization, 146, 150
Ecumenical Association of Third Word Theologians, 38–39, 54–55, 56

Emancipation, 142–43, 145
Environment, 11–12, 148
Epistemological privilege, 4, 61, 62
Ethics, 87–90, 143
Evangelization, 53, 100–101
Evolution, 83–84, 90, 121
Exodus, 63, 85, 133

Freedom, 91, 140, 141–43, 145

Gospel, 138–41, 145

Hermeneutics, 6, 86, 128
Hybridity, 150

Indigenous people, 39, 147, 149
Infant mortality, 8–9

Jesus, 65–67, 70–77
Justice trajectory, 62, 63–64, 85–86

Kingdom of God, 65–67, 71, 76, 79, 91, 99, 128, 136–37, 138–39, 143–44

Laity, 83–84, 104
Land, 9–10, 55, 101–2
Latin American Bishops Conference (CELAM), 33–36, 39, 40, 46, 47, 48–53, 59, 96
Latin American history, 14–28
Law, 63, 85, 138, 140–41
Law and Gospel, 139–41
Luke's Gospel, 65–68, 69–70, 74–77
Lutheran theology, 90–92

Malnutrition, 7–8
Martyrdom, 103

Subject Index

Marxism, *xiii*, *xiv*, 41–42, 58, 78, 79–80, 84–87, 87–88, 90–91, 103, 105–17, 148
Messiah, 64, 85

National Security theory, 45, 53, 120
New colonialism, 20–21
Nicaraguan revolution, 53–55, 59
Nonviolence, 121–22

Option for the poor, 51–52, 76, 82, 99, 147
Opus Dei, 57

Patronage system, 68–70, 74
Pentecostalism, 60, 95
Polarization, 124, 129–32, 148
Poverty, *xiv*, 1–13, 76, 80–82, 88–89, 98, 132, 146
Praxis, *xiv*, 78–92, 100, 101, 104, 115–17, 130, 148
Prophets, 2, 64, 85, 91, 133, 148

Religion, 112–13
Repression, 43–48, 55, 57–59
Rival trajectories, 127–29

Social analysis, 1, 88, 99–100, 108, 133, 148
Social Gospel, 4, 136–37, 143–45
Solentiname, 54, 98–99
Subversive memory, 76–77

Theological anthropology, 130
Theology and Liberation series, 56
Theology of the cross, 91, 143, 150
Theology of revolution, 27–28, 117–18
Theology in the Americas, 38

Vatican II, *xiii*, 26–27, 94–96
View from below, 62, 147
Violence, 102, 105–6, 117–23, 148

Women, 39, 148
World Council of Churches, 28, 29, 30, 117

www.ingramcontent.com/pod-product-compliance
Lightning Source LLC
Chambersburg PA
CBHW050817160426
43192CB00010B/1802